Twayne's English Authors Series

Sylvia E. Bowman, *Editor*

INDIANA UNIVERSITY

Sir Francis Bacon

TEAS 40

Sir Francis Bacon

By A. WIGFALL GREEN

Twayne Publishers, Inc. :: New York

Copyright © 1966 by Twayne Publishers, Inc.
All Rights Reserved

Library of Congress Catalog Card Number: 66–21749

MANUFACTURED IN THE UNITED STATES OF AMERICA

For
Zaidee Eudora Green
Splendid Scholar and Sister

Preface

Francis Bacon is to many people either God or Satan, a man of contradictions because of his varied interests and profound thought. He was, for instance, a descendant philosophically of Socrates and Plato, but his contribution to philosophy more nearly resembles that of Aristotle, whose deductive reasoning he repudiated. By such repudiation, Bacon caused the Royal Society to be founded. The oppositions in his nature came to Bacon honestly: his mother was a spiritual child of both Plato and the Puritan; his father, although holding high office, was modest and purposefully democratic; his uncle by marriage was, with Queen Elizabeth, one of the two pillars of the kingdom; his maternal grandfather was one of the great teachers and scholars of his day. From these and other relatives and friends his ambitions and ideals arose. As a person, Bacon must not be judged harshly and hastily: the charge of bribery stemmed from neglect of control over a multitude of household servants rather than from personal lack of ethics. The breach of friendship between Bacon and Robert Devereux, Earl of Essex, and between Bacon and Sir Walter Raleigh resulted from the exercise of professional duty which Bacon had sworn to perform in good conscience. These unfortunate events have been handled in a cursory manner; and no attention has been given—except to dismiss it—to the theory that Bacon wrote the works of Shakespeare and many other authors.

Bacon's works range from poor poetry to brilliant philosophic and scientific prose—and in style from the unadorned aphorism to shimmering allegory. But the student must read all of it, slowly and sympathetically, if he would understand any of it. The sole purpose of this study is to whet the appetite of the student to read every written word of this man of the Renaissance who took all knowledge to be his province and who, like the man of the modern world, would know all and be all.

A. WIGFALL GREEN

Contents

Preface
Chronology 11

Part I THE MAN

1. Clan behind the Crown, 1561–1573 17
2. My Province, All Knowledge, 1573–1593 25
3. Eat Not Your Own Heart, 1593–1603 31
4. Man of Action, 1603–1621 36
5. Fallen Satellite, 1621–1626 43

Part II THE MIND

6. Sacred and Philosophical Paraphrase 49
7. Playmaker 57
8. From Chrysalis to *Essays* 66
9. *Essays* 76
10. Apologist 88
11. A Book of Conduct for the Royalty 92
12. Biographer 98
13. *Advancement of Learning Divine and Humane* 106
14. *Cogitata et Visa* and *De Sapientia Veterum* 117
15. *Novum Organum* 125
16. *Great Renewal of Learning* 132
17. Political Strategist and Scientist 151
18. Man of Law 165
19. Scientific Utopia: *New Atlantis* 170
20. Godspeed, Francis Bacon 179

Notes and References 181
Selected Bibliography 187
Index 193

Chronology

1561 (1560 of the civil or fiscal year, which began on March 25) Francis Bacon born on January 22 at York House on the Thames River at Charing Cross, outside London; son of Sir Nicholas Bacon, Lord Keeper in reign of Queen Elizabeth I.
1573 Enrolled at Trinity College, Cambridge University.
1575 Left Cambridge University.
1576 Attaché, British embassy, Paris.
1579 Returned to England and enrolled at Gray's Inn.
1582 Became a barrister.
1584 Member of Parliament, representing Melcombe Regis.
1585 *The Greatest Birth of Time,* referred to in 1625 by Bacon as a juvenile work.
1586 Made a bencher. Member of Parliament, representing Taunton.
1588 Lent reader, or lecturer. Collaborated in *The Misfortunes of Arthur.* Member of Parliament, representing Liverpool.
1589 Granted reversion of clerkship of Star Chamber. Wrote *An Advertisement Touching the Controversies of the Church of England,* published 1640.
1592 Contributed to a triumph presented by Essex to Queen Elizabeth. Wrote *Certain Observations Made upon a Libel . . . ,* published 1593.
1593 Member of Parliament, representing Middlesex.
1594 Master of Arts degree conferred by Cambridge University. Member of Queen's Counsel of Law. Collaborated in *Gesta Grayorum.* Began *The Storehouse [Promus] of Formularies and Elegancies.* Wrote *A True Report of the Detestable Treason Intended by Dr. Roderigo Lopez,* published 1657.

1595	Contributed to a device presented by Essex to Queen Elizabeth.
1597	Publication of *Essays, Religious Meditations* [*Meditationes Sacrae*], and *Of the Colours of Good and Evil.* Selected *Maxims of the Law*, published 1630. Member of Parliament, representing Southampton.
1598	Wrote "Concerning Human Lives" [*In vitam humanam*]. Arrested for debt.
1600	*Upon the Statute of Uses*, lectures at Gray's Inn, but only published in 1642.
1601	Essex executed. Bacon wrote *A Declaration of the Practices and Treasons . . . by Robert, Late Earl of Essex.* Member of Parliament for Ipswich and St. Albans.
1603	Wrote *A Confession of Faith* this year or earlier. Elizabeth died; James I crowned. Wrote *The Goal of Valerius* [*Valerius Terminus*]. Began the *Advancement of Learning.* Published *The Happy Union of the Kingdoms of England and Scotland.* Wrote *Interpretation of Nature* [*Interpretatio Naturae*] and probably wrote *Preface to the Interpretation of Nature* [*De Interpretatione Naturae Prooemium*]. Knighted.
1604	Published *Certain Considerations Touching the Better Pacification and Edification of the Church of England*, probably written in 1603. Wrote *Certain Articles or Considerations Touching the Union of the Kingdoms of England and Scotland.* Published *Sir Francis Bacon His Apology, in Certain Imputations concerning the Late Earl of Essex.* Again member of Parliament for Ipswich and St. Albans.
1605	Published the *Advancement of Learning.*
1606	Married Alice Barnham.
1607	Made solicitor general. Probably wrote *Reflections and Speculations* [*Cogitata et Visa*] at this time.
1608	Dedicated to King James *Of the True Greatness of the Kingdom of Britain.* Succeeded to clerkship of the Star Chamber. Began the *New Instrument* [*Novum Organum*]. Wrote *In Happy Memory of Elizabeth* [*In felicem Memoriam Elizabethae*].
1609	Presented to King James *Certain Considerations Touch-*

Chronology

ing the Plantation in Ireland. Published *Concerning the Wisdom of the Ancients* [*De Sapientia Veterum*].
1610 Wrote *The Beginning of the History of Great Britain*.
1612 Second edition of the *Essays*. Wrote *Description of the World of Thought* [*Descriptio Globi Intellectualis*] and *Thesis on the Heavens* [*Thema Coeli*]. Between 1612 and 1614 wrote *New Atlantis*, published 1627.
1613 Assisted in *The Masque of the Inner Temple and Gray's Inn* by Francis Beaumont. Appointed attorney general.
1614 Presented *The Masque of Flowers*. Member of Parliament for Ipswich, St. Albans, and Cambridge University.
1616 Appointed member of the Privy Council.
1617 Appointed Lord Keeper of the Great Seal.
1618 Sir Walter Raleigh beheaded. Appointed lord chancellor. Created Baron Verulam of Verulam.
1620 Published the *New Instrument* [*Novum Organum*] and parts of the *Great Renewal of Learning* [*Instauratio Magna*].
1621 Created Viscount St. Alban. Imprisoned for bribery; released and pardoned.
1622 Published *The History of the Reign of King Henry the Seventh*. *Natural and Experimental History* [*Historia Naturalis et Experimentalis*], including *History of Winds* [*Historia Ventorum*], appeared. Published *History of Life and Death* [*Historia Vitae et Mortis*]. Wrote *An Advertisement Touching An Holy War*, published 1629.
1624 Wrote *Considerations Touching A War with Spain*, published 1629. Published in December but dated 1625 *Translation of Certain Psalms into English Verse* and *Apothegms New and Old*.
1625 King James I died; Charles I crowned. Third edition of the *Essays* published.
1626 April 9, Francis Bacon died.

PART I

The Man

Cut is the branch that might have grown full straight,
And burnèd is Apollo's laurel bough,
That sometime grew within this learnèd man.
—CHRISTOPHER MARLOWE, *Doctor Faustus*

CHAPTER 1

Clan behind the Crown, 1561–1573

FRANCIS BACON was born with a silver spoon in his mouth and a royal noose about his neck. With birth, he was enchained to his father, to his mother and his mother's father, to an illustrious uncle and aunt, and to four older brothers. Even the place of his birth, York House, an imposing but ancient structure so close to the palace at Whitehall that the royal gardens and the spacious grounds of York House formed one estate, was owned not by his father but by the nation.

I A *Noble Father*

Sir Nicholas Bacon, the father of Francis, was neighbor, friend, and faithful servant to Queen Elizabeth. He took the degree of bachelor of arts at Corpus Christi College, Cambridge University, where he was a close friend of William Cecil, later Lord Burghley, and of Matthew Parker, later archbishop of Canterbury.

At Cambridge, Nicholas held a Bible-clerkship and, in that nursery of Protestantism, confirmed his own faith. He was later said to be a man of good judgment concerning Christ's religion. He mastered the philosophy of Aristotle and the languages of the ancients and later wrote verses in Latin, including tributes to the *trivium*—or courses in the liberal arts embracing grammar, logic, and rhetoric—as well as to the *quadrivium*—or courses leading to the degree of master of arts embracing geometry, astronomy (astrology), arithmetic, and music, or the sciences emphasized by Pythagoras, Greek philosopher of the sixth century before Christ. Later in life he assiduously read the works of the Roman rhetorician Quintilian, and achieved distinction as an orator, grave and eloquent.

A son of the sheep reeve of the abbey at Bury St. Edmunds and always a humble man, Nicholas Bacon believed that learning should be shared by rich and poor alike and, so believing, founded a free grammar school for poor boys at Redgrave and established scholarships at Cambridge for their later study. He also contributed bountifully to a fund for the construction of a chapel at his college. In so honoring learning, he also honored himself.

Nicholas Bacon, decorated at eighteen with a bachelor's degree from Cambridge, went to Paris to continue his cultural education. Upon his return to England, he studied law at Gray's Inn; and, after admission to the bar, he became the solicitor for Cambridge University. The distinguished law school commanded such admiration from Nicholas that he founded a library at Gray's Inn and sent his three sons by a first marriage to Jane Fernley of Suffolk to that institution.

Under Henry VIII Nicholas prospered: in 1546 Henry appointed him attorney for the Court of Wards and Liveries; and, with the dissolution of the monasteries, Henry shared the spoils with Nicholas, including land that had belonged to the monastery at St. Albans. To this property Nicholas joined Gorhambury, near St. Albans, which he purchased in 1550. Under the reign of the Catholic queen, Mary, Nicholas could expect no advancement; but he was not exiled or persecuted, as were many other Protestant courtiers, and was permitted to continue in public office. With the return to power of the Protestants under Elizabeth in 1558, Nicholas advanced rapidly: during the first year of her reign he became a knight, a member of the privy council, and lord keeper of the great seal. As lord keeper, he had all the authority of a lord chancellor—a title usually reserved for an ecclesiast holding the great seal; he presided over the House of Lords; and he occupied York House, official residence of lord keeper or lord chancellor.

After Jane Fernley died, Nicholas Bacon married a second time, probably in 1556 or 1557. By this marriage, Nicholas yoked himself even closer to royalty, Protestantism, and learning. His second wife was Ann Cooke, a daughter of Sir Anthony Cooke. The new father-in-law of Nicholas was but four years his senior, and the new wife was eighteen years his junior.

Clan behind the Crown, 1561-1573

II A Scholarly Grandfather

Sir Anthony Cooke, a master of Greek and Latin, had been the tutor to Prince Edward and, later, to King Edward VI, as well as to his own daughter. All of his daughters married well: two married noblemen of some distinction; a third, Elizabeth, married Sir Thomas Hoby, translator of Castiglione's *The Courtier,* and, after his death, Lord Russell; a fourth, Mildred, married William Cecil, later Lord Burghley, the secretary of state. Mildred and Ann were reputed to be the most learned women in England, not excluding Queen Elizabeth.

Sir Anthony also imbued his daughters with his ardent zeal for Protestantism, a zeal further kindled by his attending the lectures of Peter Martyr, an Italian who championed the Reformation in England. To Sir Anthony, Peter Martyr dedicated his "Commentary on the Epistle to the Romans." In addition to a contribution to a translation of Demosthenes, Sir Anthony wrotes verses in Latin which were published in collections commemorative of Martin Bucer, the German reformer.

III An Erudite but Puritanical Mother

Ann Cooke acted as governess of Prince Edward when her father tutored him, and it is not improbable that she also aided in instructing the prince since she read Greek, Latin, Italian, and French as well as she read her native language. Ann, like her father, wrote memorial verses; she also translated into English various sermons and, from the Latin, Bishop John Jewel's *Apology of the Church of England.* "These being the parents," Dr. William Rawley says of Nicholas and Ann, ". . . [one] may easily imagine what the issue was like to be; having had whatsoever nature or breeding could put into him."[1] Rawley was referring to Francis Bacon, but the issue of Nicholas and Ann Bacon consisted of two sons: Anthony, born in delicate health; and Francis, born three years later and, like his brother given a single name, that of a saint.

The early education of Anthony and Francis followed, with slight variation, that of other noble sons: instruction at home by parents and private tutors; study at one of the two great universities; a trip to the Continent; service, before or after university

[19]

education, in the household of a noble friend of the family; and professional training. Ann Bacon, daughter of a royal tutor, undoubtedly contributed greatly to the early education of her sons. Sir Nicholas, like his wife, was greatly interested in the training of youth, particularly in training for the service of the nation. He had, with two other men, drafted a plan for the use of monastic revenues in instructing young men of promise in Latin and French and civil law, after which some should become specialists in national affairs and international relationships, and others should serve in embassies in foreign lands. In addition, in 1561, the date of the birth of Francis, Sir Nicholas recommended that young persons under the jurisdiction of the Court of Wards be instructed in athletics, morals, the fine arts, and literature. Undoubtedly Sir Nicholas put his educational theory into practice in the training of his sons.

IV *Dominating Uncle and Aunt*

The relatives of the immediate family who also made an impact upon the education of the boys, included their brilliant aunt, Lady Mildred Cooke Cecil. Their uncle, in his own right, was also concerned with the proper education of youth. Sir William Cecil had been taught by Sir John Cheke, university lecturer to another great schoolmaster, Roger Ascham, and tutor to Lady Jane Grey and to the prince who became Edward VI. Sir William Cecil, whose first wife was the sister of Sir John Cheke, translated Greek, Latin, Italian, and French with ease. Sir William retained tutors, probably including Dr. Richard Neile, later archbishop of York, to instruct his son Robert, a hunchback two years younger than Francis. These tutors were available to instruct Anthony and Francis Bacon. Sir Nicholas Bacon also retained private tutors, one of them, in all likelihood, being John Walsall, his chaplain.[2]

V *Escape from Learning*

In the lush gardens surrounding York House, Anthony and Francis could increase their formal education by watching the birds and insects, and the sun and moon and stars. Wandering southward along the slimy banks of the Thames River, they could feel the wind and the fog on their boyish faces and watch the tides ebb and flow, and store up memories concerning the habits

Clan behind the Crown, 1561–1573

of Nature which Francis would later try to solve. Wandering northward to the Strand, which had not yet become a street, they could mingle with the shopkeepers and fishwives and wizened women peddling fistfuls of lavender and with paupers and pickpockets—but all these people seemed to belong to another planet: they lived in the body and not in the mind. Wandering westward, more to their taste, they could stroll through the royal gardens and perchance see the regal Elizabeth taking an airing and escaping the burdens with which her courtiers in Whitehall Palace were smothering her. The glorious queen might even say to Francis, "My young Lord Keeper, how old are you?" And he would amuse the queen with his "pregnancy and towardness of wit" and a "gravity and maturity above his years" by replying, "I am two years younger than Her Majesty's happy reign." [3]

The social and political training of the boys was whetted by visits to government buildings, where they met the politicians of the inner circle and distinguished scholars. Francis made a daily call upon his father in his office, a practice continued until the death of Sir Nicholas. Anthony and Francis also spent much time at Redgrave, one of the country houses of their father, and at Burghley, one of the colossal country places of their uncle, Sir William Cecil. Both Sir Nicholas and Sir William, although each received a niggardly official salary, could well afford to entertain lavishly because of generous gifts of Queen Elizabeth's father, Henry VIII, of former monastic properties.

VI *Royal Feasts and Quips*

But Sir Nicholas was not willing to entertain the queen, accompanied by her vast royal retinue, or other distinguished guests at a place unworthy of them. When Francis was two, Sir Nicholas began to construct a new house at Gorhambury; it was completed when Francis was seven at a cost of nearly two thousand pounds, about two hundred thousand dollars in modern values. In the early 1570's Sir Nicholas several times entertained the queen at Gorhambury. But Elizabeth, difficult to please, complained of the smallness of the house. As might be expected of the father of Francis, Sir Nicholas replied, "Madam, my house is well, but it is you that have made me too great for my house." [4] Anticipating another visit from the queen, Sir Nicholas added before 1576 a gallery to the house. On a royal progress in 1577 Elizabeth made no complaint about the entertainment lasting six days and costing Sir Nicholas six hundred pounds. After the queen's departure, Sir Nicholas permanently closed the door through which the queen had entered.

The boys, Anthony and Francis Bacon and their cousin Robert Cecil, eagerly absorbed the wit and wisdom of their fathers and other noblemen; and from them they acquired skill in political chess, which demanded only flattery and chicanery. Sir William Cecil, fearful that the queen might ostracize or imprison him, and Sir Nicholas Bacon fearing that she might turn over the great seal to another, without shame fawned upon the queen and put on their best faces. "Anger makes dull men witty," Francis later says in an axiom associated with Queen Elizabeth, "but it keeps them poor." In the various versions of his *Apophthegms*, Francis recalls this period: Sir William, while entertaining the queen at Theobalds, lined up a number of his followers and asked the queen to knight them; every room at Gorhambury had running water, piped from ponds a mile distant; and Sir Nicholas, asked to evaluate two men favored by the queen, replied, "The one is a grave counsellor; the other is a proper young man, and so he will be as long as he lives."

Into the *Apophthegms*—like the courtiers in the spacious banquet hall at Gorhambury—step queen's favorites like Walter Raleigh and Sir Edward Dyer, who, seated at feast, exhibit their charm in anecdotes old and new. The queen guffawed over the earthy ones. After guzzling the beer, ale, and wine which Sir Nicholas provided liberally at a royal feast lasting six days during 1577, any one of the courtiers, upon being served chicken and capon—thirty-one dozen of the former and seventeen dozen of the latter—might have observed, as Francis records, that just as philosophers of many schools became Epicureans but Epicureans never turned to any other school, just so roosters may be made capons, but capons may never be made roosters. And Elizabeth must have been delighted with the anecdote about the old woman who could not tell the minister how many commandments there are. When the minister told her that there are ten, "Good Lord," the old woman exclaimed, "a goodly company." Then the minister asked her whether she had kept all the commandments, and she replied, "Alas, master, I am a poor woman; I have much ado to keep myself."

And so the banqueteers kept on entertaining the queen, knowing that they could not rely on hope alone to remain in her favor; for, as the axiom goes, "Hope is a good breakfast but a bad supper," and "Good fame is like fire: when you have kindled it, you may easily preserve it, but, if once you extinguish it, you will not easily kindle it again."

VII A Heavy Heritage

In this stagnant, darksome pool, lightened by the wisdom of the ancients and agitated by the competition of the courtiers, Francis Bacon learned to cower but to cherish ambition; to detect the rivalry between his father and his uncle for favor of the queen, and that between his cousin Robert and himself; and to penetrate the cat-and-mouse game that Elizabeth played in aligning each courtier against all others. In this company, Francis incubated reverence for his elders, devotion to his country, and worship of its symbol, Elizabeth.

From their mother and their aunt, Lady Mildred Cooke Cecil, Anthony and Francis Bacon acquired fondness for foreign tongues, love of learning, sharpness of speech, unbridled ambition, and uncompromising religious views passed on by the zealots of Germany and Switzerland. All these things were in their way of good influence; but they were also bad. Both boys were of weak constitution—Anthony permanently lamed and, at fourteen, threatened with loss of vision; and Francis bedridden for extended periods throughout his life—his health was made worse by constant study. Both boys had to learn that concealment of aggressiveness is often a prerequisite to success; and both had to elevate themselves from the valley of Detestants, a term used in the *Apophthegms,* to the hills of liberal Protestants. But their task was to liberate themselves from the domination of their mother, who unconsciously stifled their libidos by treating them throughout their lives as though they were mere boys in their pre-teens.

From their father, "a man plain, direct, and constant," they acquired a show, at least, of simplicity and frankness and the qualities of the contemplative man—characteristics opposed to the qualities of the active man derived from their mother.[5] Unfortunately, however, they learned from their father that the thought of Aristotle is unchallengeable; that their nation was, and ever must be, the greatest nation in the world; and that before the crown they must genuflect and submerge their will and their intelligence in the will and intelligence of the queen.

The Bacon boys had to recognize the law of the pendulum and to memorize the maxim—like all other proverbs, not entirely true—that "Violent action creates equally violent reaction." The brilliance of their parents benefited and benighted them; the fondness and the fickleness of Queen Elizabeth comforted and smothered them; the confines of their island paradise ennobled and strait-jacketed them. Hard would be the path to the knowledge that an island is smaller than the universe, an individual than man, and a man than nature.

CHAPTER 2

My Province, All Knowledge, 1573–1593

IN 1573 Bacon was a boy of twelve; in 1593, at thirty-two, he was a man who had thought deeply and had experienced many things. At Cambridge University he challenged the philosophy tailored by Aristotle; accepted the new scientific discoveries; and, journeying beyond, without laboratory equipment or sound training in science, began a personal study of the mysteries of Nature. In France, escaping from the embassy close, he continued experiments. More important, he studied the French people and their language, and he gave earnest attention to the politics and the religions of France. Upon his return to England, he studied not only the laws of England but the reason, or the philosophy, behind them. In Parliament he applied to his speeches on national issues the profound thought that he had devoted to the problems and the liberality that he had acquired.

Bacon's background followed him during the experiences of these two decades, but he revolted against that background. His older brother went with him to Cambridge; but, as a student, Francis overshadowed his brother. His father's judiciousness was ever with Francis, but the son learned to penetrate more deeply into science and law and philosophy than his father had the capacity or daring to penetrate. To France he took the puritanism of his mother, but there he gained a new respect for more liberal religion and for a political system which recognized minority groups. There also and in Parliament he began to question the dogma that the will of the queen is superior to reason.

I   *Cambridge University*

Informal study completed for the two sons by his second marriage, Sir Nicholas in April, 1573, sent them to Trinity College, Cambridge University, where once again Anthony and Francis shared the learning of men. Francis, but twelve, was well prepared for college study. Anthony and Francis, who shared quarters, were placed under the mastership of Dr. John Whitgift, later archbishop of Canterbury, a close friend of Sir Nicholas.

The language requirement at Trinity was no problem for Francis even though students were required except when in quarters or at leisure to speak in Hebrew, Greek, or Latin. His later works reveal an interest in Hebrew; he translated from Greek to English and often used Greek characters in messages to his mother and other persons; and he collected axioms and corresponded in Latin, and sometimes wrote or had his writing translated into that tongue for his approval.

Pleased with the work in language at Trinity, Francis was just as much displeased with the work in science which at the time was embraced by philosophy, of which Aristotle was the master. Francis soon "fell into the dislike of the philosophy of Aristotle" because of his "unfruitfulness." Such philosophy, young Francis thought, was "strong for disputations and contentions, but barren of the production of works for the benefit of the life of man, in which mind he continued to his dying day." [1] Nature herself had belied Aristotle: he had insisted that the region of Cassiopeia was unalterable, but a new star appeared in that region in 1572 and was extinguished in 1574.

Trinity College, Francis soon learned, was dominated by politics and religion. Even admirable persons like Dr. Whitgift, "a prelate of the first magnitude for sanctity, learning, patience, and humility," could not satisfy the intellectual hunger of the lad.[2] In the first book of the *Advancement of Learning,* Bacon later condemned schoolmasters like Roger Ascham who "almost deify Cicero and Demosthenes" and cause "the learning of the schoolmen to be utterly despised as barbarous" because they shut up their wits "in the cells of a few authors (chiefly Aristotle their dictator) as their persons were shut up in the cells of monasteries and colleges." [3]

Illness interrupted the education of the boys. Anthony had recurrent illness between 1573 and 1575; and the plague, raging from August, 1574, to March, 1575, kept both of them at home, probably at Gorhambury, during that period. At Christmas, 1575, Anthony and Francis withdrew from Cambridge without the degree, probably a source of disappointment to their father, who had received the degree of bachelor of arts and had become the solicitor of the university. During the brief periods that Anthony and Francis had resided at Trinity College, they had learned a great deal; and Francis had commanded respect as "more than an ordinary proficient in the several arts and sciences."[4] At Cambridge, Francis' only known experiment in science was in sound: an upper chamber of one of the buildings at Trinity College had been provided with a central pillar of iron to support a weak roof; when the pillar was struck, it made "a little flat noise" in that room but it gave off "a great bomb in the chamber beneath."[5]

II *The Young Diplomat*

Francis made further experiments in sound in a stimulating new world. Sir Nicholas Bacon believed that the primary education of boys of superior background and ability should be for statecraft and that such training should include service in a British embassy abroad. With the appointment of his friend, Sir Amias Paulet, to the ambassadorship to France, he, therefore, arranged with Paulet to include Francis as an embassy attaché. Only fifteen, Francis took his first and last voyage abroad in 1576. Near the Seine in a chapel with but four walls and two rows of pillars remaining, Francis spoke a word at one end and found that the voice returned thirteen times, each return being weaker than the last. When three were spoken, all three returned three times; then the last two words returned "some times"; and finally the last word alone returned "some times, still fading and growing weaker."[6]

Exploring the countryside, Francis traveled from Paris to Blois, to Tours, and to Poitiers where a witty young Frenchman enthralled him with the notion that the physical defects of old men reflect themselves in mental and spiritual defects: bleared eyes in envy; clutching of the fingers in avarice; and wrinkles in crooked ways.[7] The youth, while perfecting his French, was garnering ideas for later writings.

Upon the return of Francis to Paris, the ambassador sent him back to England with diplomatic correspondence for Queen Elizabeth, who was concerned, among many other things, with the state of religion in France. Situated between Protestantism in the north and Catholicism in the south, France itself consisted of three politico-religious groups: the Protestants, the Catholics, and the *Politiques* who were in essence Catholic but responsive to Protestant demands which might preclude struggle within the nation. Sir Amias, a zealous Puritan, undoubtedly advised Elizabeth on religion and the flux of politics in France; and Francis undoubtedly served as an able interpreter.

Upon his return to Paris, Francis devised a secret code of writing, or cipher, consisting of the enfoldment of each letter of the alphabet, except *j* and *u*, in twenty-four combinations of *a* and *b*: *a*, for example, is enfolded in *aaaaa*, *m* in *ababb*, and *z* in *babbb*.[8] In the later work in which he gives an account of the cipher, he reveals his interest in phonetics and his facility in dealing with foreign language: Greek abounds in diphthongs, of which Latin is much more sparing; Spanish avoids thin letters, and changes them to middle tone; and the Gothic languages are copious in aspirates.[9]

France gave to the boy rich experience in living and learning. But the boy Francis was violently transmuted to the man Bacon by a dream that his "father's house in the country was plastered all over with black mortar."[10] A few days later he learned that, in February, 1579, his father had died. The next month Francis left Paris for England, and he bore with him a letter from the ambassador recommending him for the queen's service.

III *Law Student*

The queen's service had no important post for a young man without a large private income or, in lieu thereof, handsomeness and personal charm which appealed to Elizabeth. Sir Nicholas had planned to create an estate for his youngest son as he had done for the other four sons, but death issued a *habeas corpus* for his unwieldy body before he could invest the large sum which he had put aside for the purchase of land for the support of Francis: Sir Nicholas, as he sat by an open window after a heavy snowfall and freeze, followed by unseasonably warm weather for February, fell asleep as his barber shampooed his head. Awaking "all distempered and in great sweat," the lord keeper asked his barber why he had let him sleep. "Why, my Lord," replied the barber, "I durst not wake your Lordship," to which Sir Nicholas lamented,

My Province, All Knowledge, 1573–1593

"Why, then, you have killed me with kindness."[11] Within a few days he died, leaving to Francis a fifth of the relatively small fortune that remained after the creation of estates for the other four sons.

At eighteen, without fortune, without physical attractiveness, and without profession, young Bacon had to make a choice. A life of philosophic contemplation? Such life required a large income. A life of action in which he could make money and achieve worldly fame? Yes, that seemed to be the proper course. Having been accorded the honorary distinction—with his four brothers, as sons of a justice—of admission to membership in "the grand company" of Gray's Inn, and naturally desiring to follow the path taken by his father, Bacon turned to the serious study of the law at Gray's Inn, which remained one of his many homes from 1579 until his death.

At first he lived in the chambers earlier occupied by his father. Later he built chambers above the library. After his rise at court, five buildings took one of his titles, "Verulam Buildings." But Bacon not only built; he also planted: with the consent and financial aid of other students, he converted outlying fields into an Eden of blooming flowers and luxuriant trees. Even today the guest is shown a tree, the gift of Sir Walter Raleigh, planted by Bacon with his own hands.

At Gray's, Bacon "carried himself with such sweetness, comity, and generosity that he was much revered and beloved by the readers and gentlemen of the house."[12] He rose rapidly, in 1582 becoming an utter barrister (one admitted to the practice of the law) and in 1586 a bencher (one entitled to practice in the courts of Westminster). Soon thereafter he became a reader, or lecturer, at Gray's Inn.

IV Member of Parliament

Experience as a lawyer and lecturer in the law, as well as a desire to serve the crown, encouraged Bacon to enter politics. He represented Melcombe Regis in Parliament in 1584; Taunton, in 1586; Liverpool, in 1589; and Middlesex, in 1593. He was both active and articulate in behalf of the crown, but he gave offense to Elizabeth in the last Parliament by speaking against excessive subsidy. When the door to advancement was slammed in his face, Bacon said that he had spoken out of duty to God, queen, and country.

The link with Parliament was also a link with the crown, a link which Bacon desired to tighten. On several occasions he importuned his uncle to aid him in obtaining a post at the royal court. When, in 1585 at the age of twenty-four, he was told that he was too young to be appointed to any important post, he sadly commented that the objection to his years would wear off with the years seemingly required to make such appointment. To salve his smart, the queen in 1589 granted to him the reversion to the clerkship of the Star Chamber, a remunerative office but one which did not come into possession for two decades, much too late to aid him in immediate financial straits. His appetite for high position still unslaked, Bacon in 1592 wrote to Sir William Cecil of his continued desire to serve the queen. "I have taken," he says, "all knowledge to be my province." [13]

CHAPTER 3

Eat Not Your Own Heart, 1593–1603

THE decade 1593–1603 is distinguished by Bacon's literary output and by his attempts to win the favor of friends who might help to advance him at the royal court. He continued to implore the aid of his uncle until the death of Sir William Cecil, first Baron Burghley, in 1598. He sought aid also through the son of Sir William, Sir Robert Cecil, who had become the queen's principal secretary. Francis also turned to his brother Anthony, who, until his death in 1601, was engaged by Essex to collect intelligence in Scotland and in Europe—intelligence to counter the intelligence being collected by the Cecils on their own behalf and on behalf of the queen. From the camp of the Cecils, Francis turned, from time to time, to that of Essex, even to the extent that he placed his brother Anthony in the espionage force of Essex. During this decade also a rivalry with Sir Edward Coke, begun in 1593 and continued until Bacon's death, burned at white heat.

I *Sir William Cecil*

Sir William Cecil was more a father than an uncle by marriage to Francis. While Francis was a law student, Sir William interceded with the queen for a legal position for his nephew; he promoted the rapid advance of Francis at Gray's Inn; he obtained for him the reversion to the clerkship of the Star Chamber; and, in 1594, he procured for him membership in the Learned Counsel of the crown, an appointment without patent or fixed salary and with intermittent duties only, but, nevertheless, an important appointment. After the first appearance of Francis as an attorney in the King's Bench, his Uncle William sent him congratulations and requested notes on the case in order that he might use them to the best advantage of his nephew. And Sir William was happy when his nephew received the degree of master of arts at Cambridge

University, even though Francis, refusing to be immersed in the mass arranged for a special congregation to grant the degree to him, but to no other person, on July 27, 1594. Francis, in turn, defended his uncle by writing against various libels, including the charge that Sir William endeavored to pre-empt public offices for his sons.

When, in 1593, Bacon heard the rumor that the attorney general was to be promoted, he decided to use influence to obtain the attorney generalship and thereby exclude Sir Edward Coke, the solicitor general, who expected to be promoted. Bacon turned not to Sir William but to his son by a first marriage, Sir Thomas Cecil, and asked him to obtain the recommendation of his father. He likewise asked Sir Robert Cecil to request the help of his father. Sir Thomas, commending the ability of Bacon, urged the support of his father; but Sir Robert replied that Bacon should press the Earl of Essex for the appointment. Bacon then wrote to the queen: "But if any of my friends do press this matter, I do assure your Majesty my spirit is not with them." [1] Sir William—"the old fox," Anthony designated him—did not recommend Francis for the attorney generalship but did support him for the solicitor generalship after Sir Edward Coke received the attorney generalship in 1594.[2] Bacon was better qualified for the solicitorship than any of his competitors, but Coke would not submit to the appointment of Bacon as second in command of the legal office of the crown.

II *Sir Edward Coke*

Bacon's recognition of Coke's superior qualifications for the office of attorney general deepened the rift between the two men. Bacon was relatively young, nine years younger than Coke; he had little experience in the law courts, although he had achieved some distinction as a lecturer; and his absorption in the philosophy of the law had given him contempt for memorization and rapid recitation of statutes and precedents, a field in which Coke was a master.

Bacon's hope of receiving an important legal post dashed, he determined to get ahead at the royal court through marriage. The best prospect was in his own family, Lady Hatton, the widow of Sir William Hatton and the daughter of his own half cousin, Sir Thomas Cecil. Young, intelligent, beautiful, and very rich, Lady

Eat Not Your Own Heart, 1593-1603

Hatton would make a perfect wife. But Lady Hatton had another suitor to whom she was reputed to be engaged, Sir Foulke Greville, a cousin of Robert Devereux, Earl of Essex. Perhaps because of the rumored engagement or, more likely, as Bacon says in his essay "Of Friendship," because "A man can scarce allege his own merits with modesty, much less extol them," Bacon asked Devereux to place in his hands letters of commendation addressed to Lady Hatton, to her mother, and to her father. Devereux yielded and wrote highly complimentary letters. But in 1598 Lady Hatton startled English society by marrying not Bacon or Greville but a man uncouth, domineering, and greedy—Sir Edward Coke.

III *Robert Devereux, Second Earl of Essex*

The affection of Sir William Cecil for his nephews, Anthony and Francis Bacon, cannot be questioned. In 1593 he wrote extolling their virtue and learning to their mother. But Sir William's prudence made him reluctant to endorse the request of Francis for the attorney generalship. Francis, following the suggestion of his cousin, Sir Robert Cecil, and his own inclination, sought, therefore, the aid of the Earl of Essex, whose acquaintance he had made about 1591.

Essex, when only seven, was placed by his father under the guardianship of Sir William Cecil with the request that the boy be married to Anne, the daughter of Sir William. Essex was not only related by blood to various distinguished courtiers, but the cousin of his grandmother was Queen Elizabeth, who was thirty-four years his senior. The political bond between Elizabeth and the Cecils was close, but the blood bond with Essex even closer. Elizabeth was also attracted to the boy's brilliance: at ten, he was a master of English, Latin, and French; and, at eleven, he entered Trinity College, Cambridge University, where, like the Bacon brothers, he was under the tutelage of Whitgift. But the boy, like the rest of his family, was self-willed. At eleven, he refused to doff his cap in the queen's presence; moreover, he declined her proposal that he kiss her. Any association between two such high-spirited persons was doomed to be stormy.

Essex, impressed by the genius of Bacon, immediately championed his request for the attorney generalship; but, unfortunately for Bacon, he approached the queen through her secretary, Sir

Robert Cecil. When Cecil told Essex that the queen might have honored a request for the solicitor generalship but not for the higher office, Essex charged the Cecils with seeking preferment for a stranger rather than for their near kinsman. When the attorney generalship was given to Coke, Essex zealously sought the solicitorship for Bacon—so zealously that he aroused the wrath of the queen toward him and toward Bacon. When the solicitorship also was lost to Bacon, Essex, with typical generosity, gave his friend a tract of land which Bacon later sold for one thousand eight hundred pounds.

Anthony Bacon, who in 1579 had begun an extended tour of Europe to collect information for the Cecils, entered in 1593 the intelligence service of Essex and undertook to gather news concerning potential enemies prior to its collection by other agents of the queen. Essex, known to favor the succession of James VI of Scotland to the English throne, directed Anthony also to assemble intelligence in Scotland.

Essex, always self-incited to gain military glory, was moderately pleased with his success against the Spanish Armada; but he was ill-advised to undertake an expedition to subdue Hugh O'Neill, the Earl of Tyrone, who had rebelled against the British forces in Ireland. Francis Bacon protested his going to Ireland, but the headstrong Essex was not to be dissuaded. Dissatisfied with logistical support and disregarding the orders of the queen to remain in Ireland, Essex returned with a band of officers and men to make a personal demand upon the queen. Elizabeth, having received Essex graciously, deviously ordered him confined to his chamber. On June 5, 1600, Essex was given a judicial hearing; and Bacon, as a member of the royal judicial service, was assigned the distasteful duty of charging Essex with having displeased the queen, but not of disloyalty or treason. Essex was relieved of public office and made a prisoner in his own house at the will of the queen. In a letter which Bacon sent to Essex on July 20, 1600, he said that in a conflict of loyalties he preferred the good of his country to the friendship of Essex.

With a following of but three hundred men, Essex escaped from his house on February 8, 1601, and attempted to seize the Tower of London and the royal guard; but he was forced to return in defeat to Essex House. On February 11, Bacon was commissioned to examine the conspirators; and Essex was arraigned on February 20. Even though Coke blundered in prosecuting the case, Essex was found guilty and was promptly executed.

In submission to an order of the queen that Bacon allay popular misunderstanding by writing an exposition of the case, he sent to the press on April 14, 1601, his *Declaration of the Practices and Treasons Attempted and Committed by Robert Late Earl of Essex and His Complices*. In 1604, once again endeavoring to lay the ghost of Essex, he published *Sir Francis Bacon His Apologie, in Certain Imputations concerning the Late Earle of Essex* in which he says courageously that "every honest man . . . will forsake his King rather than forsake God, and forsake his friend rather than forsake his King." As a member of the royal judicial staff, Bacon received no regular or fixed compensation; but he was awarded for his services in the Essex case one thousand two hundred pounds by the crown.

IV An End Makes a Beginning

Worn out in his service of nearly forty years as secretary of state, Sir William Cecil died in 1598. Bewailing his "infectious sin," Essex was executed in 1601; and immediately thereafter the executioner held aloft the head of Essex and shouted, "God save the Queen!" Three months later Anthony Bacon, still loyal to Essex, died. Elizabeth shorn of her trusted secretary of state and her spirited young kinsman, could not long be saved. Withering in her loneliness, she died at the age of seventy on March 24, 1603.

Instinctively Bacon turned from the death behind him to the life before him. The new king, James I of England, left Edinburgh on April 5 for London; and Bacon met him on the way. A man cannot eat out his own heart for what is past or for what is dead.

CHAPTER 4

Man of Action, 1603–1621

WITH the coming of King James in 1603, Bacon entered the fourth important period of his life. He had freed himself of the clan which had enchained him during the first period, 1561–73; with the few remaining Bacons, he had no strong ties. Of the Cookes, his mother yet lived; but her religious zeal had turned to madness. Of the Cecils, only Sir Robert remained; and he was to die midway in the new period. Bacon had also passed through the second stage, 1573–93, one in which he had garnered knowledge which he was now able to put to practical use. And he had profited from the third decade, 1593–1603, in which he had engaged the enemy in battle—and had lost. He was still a bachelor, still hungering for position; he had nothing to lose but much to gain.

During the eighteen years of the fourth period, 1603–21, although Bacon produced his most important philosophical and scientific works, he devoted equal effort to seeking for himself; and during this period, sharply contrasted to the third period, he gained all that which he had earlier sought in vain—and much more than even he had been able to envision. The facts of this period are so well known that they can be covered with little detail.

I *King James I of England*

The similarities between James I and Bacon gave rise to an immediate rapport. James, like Essex, was five years the junior of Bacon; and, like Essex, James could appreciate the worth of the man and could accept instruction by him. James, having become the king of Scotland when only one year old, had been, like Bacon, nurtured in a gentle manner and tutored by the most learned scholars of his nation. Both men were, in physical appearance, less

Man of Action, 1603-1621

than attractive; both were ceremonious; both were—to use a word from James's vocabulary—"pawky," or sly or humorous. Both spoke and wrote well, James quaintly and Bacon brilliantly; both preferred to negotiate through intermediaries and not directly; both were philosophic and both were—or appeared to be—deeply religious; both were fervid to unite the religions of the two nations, and to unite the nations themselves. The affinity between the two men, each representing the most enlightened thought of his nation, was spontaneous.

II Swift Rise

"The canvassing world is gone," Bacon wrote to a friend immediately after the arrival of James, "and the deserving world is come."[1] To a cousin he wrote, "As the State here hath performed the part of good attorneys to deliver the King quiet possession of his kingdom, so the King will redeliver them quiet possession of their places."[2] Bacon was retained as an attorney in the learned council; even better, although he had never been sworn in or held a warrant under Elizabeth as a member of the council, King James officially made him a member of that body.

With a new reign, a man with prospects must have money. Bacon was not only bankrupt but deeply indebted: he had incurred a debt of seven thousand four hundred pounds and had inherited from his brother Anthony a debt of two thousand six hundred pounds. Lack of funds was not a matter of concern except in that it limited further borrowing. Marriage, he thought, was the best escape from financial worries. To his cousin, Sir Robert, to whom he owed money which he could not pay, he turned with two additional problems. "Because I have found out an alderman's daughter, an handsome maiden, to my liking . . . I could . . . be content to have . . . this . . . almost prostituted title of knighthood."[3] But, preferring to receive the honor individually, he would "not be merely gregarious in a troop."[4] Sir Robert, now the Earl of Salisbury, interceded for the hand of Alice Barnham, the alderman's daughter; but even he met with no success for three years. With the knighthood, Salisbury was more successful: Bacon was knighted on July 23, 1603—ironically, with three hundred others. In May, 1606, Alice was married to Francis. Although she

[37]

was reputed to be sharp of tongue, Alice was the stepdaughter of Sir John Pakington, who gave a splendid wedding dinner in honor of his youthful relative and coheir of the estate of her father. The groom, though forty-five, was clad in purple. He had bestowed upon the bride raiment of cloth of silver and gold that cut deep into her dowry.

Bacon, although avid of immediate advancement through personal appeal to the king, realized that literary production would appeal equally to James. Such writing, however, must not be confined to the present; some of it must be good for all ages. "My ambition now I shall only put upon my pen," he wrote to Salisbury just after the arrival of James, "whereby I shall be able to maintain memory and merit of the times succeeding." [5] For "times succeeding" during the first year of the reign of James he wrote *The Goal of Valerius* [*Valerius Terminus*], *of the Interpretation of Nature; Interpretation of Nature* [*Interpretatio Naturae*]; and probably *Preface to the Interpretation of Nature;* and he began *The Two Books of Francis Bacon of the Proficiency and Advancement of Learning, Divine and Human*, published in 1605. But, as a matter of political expediency, he published during 1603 *A Brief Discourse Touching the Happy Union of the Kingdoms of England and Scotland* and in the following year *Certain Considerations Touching the Better Pacification and Edification of the Church of England*.

Bacon's dual appeal, personal and literary, succeeded. Passed over for promotion more than once, he was appointed on June 25, 1607, to the office of solicitor general, a position on which he placed an evaluation of a thousand pounds. In this year he produced a work for the future, *Reflections and Speculations* [*Cogitata et Visa*].

His literary production for the next three years was intended for the present and the future: in 1608, when he succeeded to the clerkship of the Star Chamber, he published *Of the True Greatness of the Kingdom of Britain*, dedicated to King James, and *In Happy Memory of Elizabeth* [*In felicem Memoriam Elizabethae*]. But he also undertook a work for the future, *New Instrument* [*Novum Organum*]. In 1609, for the present he wrote *Certain Considerations Touching the Plantation in Ireland. Presented to His Majesty;* and for the future he published *Concerning the Wisdom of*

Man of Action, 1603-1621

the Ancients [*De Sapientia Veterum*]. In 1610 he pleased the king with *The Beginning of the History of Great Britain*.

Bacon's only distinguished work prior to the coming of James was the *Essays*, first published in 1597. In 1612 the second, and most important, edition appeared. During the latter year he wrote two works for future ages: *Description of the World of Thought* [*Descriptio Globi Intellectualis*] and *Thesis on the Heavens* [*Thema Coeli*], a treastise on astronomy.

Bacon's writing, revealing the man of contemplation, aided the man of action. Although he had served as a member of Parliament since 1584, he had held no important public office except that of solicitor general. In 1613, he became the attorney general. The following year he represented in Parliament St. Albans, Ipswich, and Cambridge University. Between 1612 and 1614 he wrote his most imaginative work the *New Atlantis*, in which he combined poet, dramatist, philosopher, and scientist.

To obtain the attorney generalship, Bacon had to play politics like a professional chess player. Upon the death of the chief justice of the king's bench, he recommended to the king that the attorney general be appointed to the chief justiceship of the court of common pleas, a lucrative post held by Sir Edward Coke, Bacon's ancient rival, and that Coke be transferred to the chief justiceship of the king's bench, a position of more distinction but one paying only half as much. The king accordingly made the shifts. Coke left the common pleas in such a shower of tears that the king made him a member of the privy council in November, 1613.

Bacon was not to be outdistanced by Coke. He appealed to the king to appoint him to the office of lord chancellor, or lord keeper of the great seal—as the incumbent was often designated if not a member of the clergy. The king offered Bacon a choice between membership in the privy council and the position of lord chancellor in the event of the death of the incumbent chancellor. The chancellor, who had been ill, recovered; Bacon was made in June, 1616, a member of the privy council. Upon the resignation of the lord chancellor in March, 1617, Bacon was made lord keeper, a position which his father had held; but in January, 1618, he was made lord chancellor. Further honor was bestowed upon him: in July, 1618, his title became "Baron Verulam of Verulam."

Ever prodigal of expenditure, Bacon's new title required him, he believed, to live even more lavishly. The maintenance of the house at Gorhambury, taken over from his brother Anthony, required at least fifty servants. At York House, his birthplace on which he had obtained a lease for life, he supported a staff of at least a hundred servants, including four butlers, six gentlemen of the chambers, and more than twenty gentlemen waiters. "Who is the king," the people asked, "Francis or James?"

III *Sir Walter Raleigh*

In the popular mind, unfamiliar with the judicial system of the period, only one blemish of this time remains upon Bacon's character: his minor connection with the execution of Sir Walter Raleigh. Queen Elizabeth had leaned heavily upon Raleigh, and they had become close friends and allies in statecraft. The evidence gathered immediately before the decapitation of the Earl of Essex makes it clear that Essex had plotted to murder Elizabeth and also Raleigh. Raleigh was not, however, a favorite of King James. Immediately after the death of Elizabeth, a conference, it is said, was held to determine what should be done about the succession. Sir Walter reputedly favored the establishment of a commonwealth, an act which would preclude the subjection of England to the beggarly Scotland. That Raleigh made such a proposal is highly improbable, but it is almost certain that King James I heard that he did. In 1603, soon after the accession of James, various Catholics and Puritans combined in a plot to dethrone James and to place Lady Arabella Stuart on the throne. Raleigh was tried for high treason because of alleged complicity. Imprisoned in the Tower of London for thirteen years, he refused to languish but engaged in experiments in chemistry and began his *History of the World*. Bacon had nothing to do with the examination or sentencing of Raleigh.

Through the mediation of his friends, Raleigh was released in 1616 and was permitted to sail to South America with the understanding that he would bring back to James a half ton of gold and that, if he attacked the Spaniards in that area, he should forfeit his life. In 1617 he embarked on his perilous expedition. He failed to find gold, and he engaged in battle with the Spaniards, a battle in

Man of Action, 1603-1621

which his son, Captain Raleigh, was slain. Upon his return in August, 1618, he was again imprisoned in the Tower of London.

Bacon was appointed one of several commissioners, including the archbishop of Canterbury, to report on the case to the king. The commission urged the king to permit Raleigh to be heard before the council of state and the principal judges, but the king rejected the recommendation. Raleigh was given a hearing before his examiners and was executed in October, 1618. Public feeling became so high because of the execution that an official declaration of the offenses of Raleigh was written and published, and Bacon was one of the authors. The public, displeased with the declaration, became antagonistic toward every person, including Bacon, who had shared in the hearing and execution of Raleigh.

IV Sir George Villiers, Duke of Buckingham

Bacon also gained some unpopularity through his estrangement from Sir George Villiers, the king's favorite. The close friendship between Villiers and the king required Bacon to be diplomatic in his relationship with the duke. When, for instance, he forwarded to the king in 1616 the patent for the elevation of the favorite to Viscount Villiers, he praised the nature, mind, will, affections, and courage of the man. But real animosity began to reveal itself when Bacon attempted to control the abuse of granting monopolies. Two of the most pernicious monopolists were related to Villiers. One of them, a half brother, held the monopoly for the manufacture and sale of gold and silver thread, which was in great demand at this time, and also the patent for the licensing of alehouses. Bacon incurred the wrath of Buckingham when he urged him to gain a good reputation for abolishing monopolies rather than an evil one for maintaining them. There is no wrath like that of a king's favorite.

V Pompous Elevation

Outwardly glorious but inwardly grieved, Bacon gazed into the future and wrote, and published in 1620, *New Instrument* [*Novum Organum*] and *Preparation for a Natural and Experimental History* [*Parasceve ad Historiam Naturalem et Experimentalem*].

Some days before his birthday, tentative arrangements were

made to bestow upon Bacon the greatest honor of his life. Five days after his birthday he was created Viscount St. Albans with all the ceremonies of robes and coronet. He thanked the king for enabling him to be buried in St. Alban's vestment. To celebrate Bacon's sixtieth birthday, January 22, 1561, Ben Jonson wrote a poem of ten couplets ending:

> Give me a deep-crown'd Bowle, that I may sing
> In raysing him the wisdome of my King.

CHAPTER 5

Fallen Satellite, 1621–1626

THE stages in Bacon's life are like those of many other men: forty-six years of struggle to achieve distinction, only to meet with frustration; fourteen years of success and vacuous happiness; and five years of infirmity, a lonely outcast. Bacon's span of life was that of the ordinary man of today, sixty-five years; but his life was anything but ordinary.

The end was as extraordinary as the beginning, an end in which there was no regret for what had passed—merely a frank statement and acceptance of what had passed. Upon his downfall Bacon physically became a frail pilgrim, but intellectually he remained a robust pioneer who turned once again to the history of England, to the history of Nature, and to the epigrams uniting the ancient world and the contemporary world. He always belonged, and will always belong, to both worlds.

I *Wrath of Favorites*

Bacon's reputation with King James had been on the wane since 1617 when he had disagreed with the Duke of Buckingham about monopolies held by persons related to the duke. In addition, Bacon had offended Sir Ralph Winwood, the king's secretary. When he saw Winwood beating his dog, Bacon rebuked him by saying, "Every gentleman does love a dog." At another time, when Winwood sat too close to Bacon, he told him "either to keep or to know his distance." [1]

Even worse for Bacon was his intervention in the negotiations of Sir Edward Coke for the marriage of his daughter Frances, then fourteen, to Sir John Villiers, the brother of Buckingham—negotiations the more sensitive because Coke haggled over a long period of time concerning the large dowry which the Villiers family demanded. Neither Lady Elizabeth Hatton, as Coke's wife was still called, nor Frances had given consent to the proposed union; and Lady Hatton spirited her daughter away and hid her in a country house. Coke, accompanied by his fighting son Clem and a band of servants, broke down the door and dragged away the screaming girl. Bacon issued a warrant to Lady Hatton for the recovery of her daughter. Buckingham rebuked Bacon for overtroubling himself about the match and for conducting himself with scorn toward his friends. The king, irate on behalf of his favorite, told Bacon in a letter of late August, 1617, that "the thefteous stealing away of the daughter from her own father" was the root of the trouble, and he damned Bacon for not issuing a warrant to Coke for the recovery of the daughter and accused him of being jealous of Buckingham.[2]

II. *Charges, Trial, and Penalties*

While members of the Parliament were giving consideration to abuses of the monopolists, the House of Commons on February 28, 1621, decided to send a message to the House of Lords concerning corruption by a "man of quality." A committee on grievances was appointed, but it turned its attention from monopolies to malfeasance in the courts, especially in the chancery court. John Churchill, one of Bacon's subordinates, confessed to perjury but said that Bacon himself had accepted gratuities. The case was sent to the House of Lords. Two litigants in Bacon's court testified that, through their attorney, Sir George Hastings, they had sent money to Bacon. On March 25, Bacon told the king: "I hope I shall not be found to have the troubled fountain of a corrupt heart in a depraved habit of taking rewards to pervert justice; howsoever I may be frail, and partake of the abuse of the times." [3]

Bacon knew only too well "the abuse of the times." King James had accepted four thousand pounds from Bacon's successor in the office of attorney general, and Bacon's opponent for the position of chancellor had offered James thirty thousand pounds for that place. Buckingham had accepted twenty thousand pounds for granting the office of lord treasurer. "The abuse of the times" does not extenuate Bacon's fault, but it must be considered in judging him; and, in light of the fact that it was accepted practice for the king to demand rich rewards for bestowing titles, it raises the

Fallen Satellite, 1621–1626

question of whether Bacon had paid for appointment to public office and for noble titles, and, if so, how much and to whom.

The number of charges brought against Bacon finally reached twenty-eight. Many of the alleged bribes Bacon considered to be gifts; for mediation between litigants he had accepted money, but without previous agreement for such payment and only after cases had been adjudicated; and sometimes his numerous servants had received gifts for him of which he had no knowledge. The House of Lords found him guilty and assessed a fine of forty thousand pounds; imprisonment in the Tower of London during the king's pleasure; and disqualification to sit in Parliament, hold public office, or enter the verge of the court.[4] From the Tower of London, Bacon wrote to Buckingham on May 31, 1621: "Procure the warrant for my discharge this day."[5] On June 4, he was freed. On October 17, the king pardoned him; but the pardon excepted the penalties recently adjudged by Parliament.

Buckingham, longing for a residence in keeping with his position, demanded the sale to him of Bacon's interest in York House. Bacon temporized by dangling before the eyes of the favorite the possibility of Gorhambury as a gift; but Bacon had to yield and, as a reward for relinquishing York House, he was suffered to enter the verge.

III *Preparation for Death and Perpetuity*

Having completed his work on apothegms and psalms, Bacon mused upon death and drafted his will, published on December 19, 1625. In it he reaffirms gifts to his wife, but in a codicil he revokes all devises and bequests made in the will to Lady Bacon, probably because she had sorely displeased him. Her early remarriage after Lord Bacon's death further suggests marital infidelity. Unusual for the day, Bacon in his will directs that copies of his works be placed in the libraries of Oxford and Cambridge universities and in other libraries. Like Shakespeare, he leaves money to friends for the purchase of memorial rings. He endows scholarships for needy students at the two universities. "For my name and memory," he says in his will, "I leave it to men's charitable speeches, and to foreign nations, and the next ages." He had, however, little but his name and memory to leave; for, upon his death nearly four months later, his debts were in excess of twenty-two thousand pounds and his assets but little more than seven thousand pounds.

Just as Bacon devoted much of his life to experimenting with Nature, just so his death was brought about by such experiment: to establish the efficacy of cold in arresting putrefaction, he left his coach on a chilly day and bought a fowl which he stuffed with snow which had just fallen. Weakened by the dampness, he went to the home of a friend who had gone away and was put to bed by a servant in an unheated room. In that house he did his last writing—a letter to his friend thanking him for the hospitality of the servant and telling him of the experiment, which "succeeded excellently well."

On Easter Sunday, April 9, 1626, Bacon died. He was later buried, as he had requested in his will, in St. Michael's Church, near St. Albans, where his mother lay.

PART II

The Mind

How am I glutted with conceit of this!
Shall I make spirits fetch me what I please,
Resolve me of all ambiguities,
Perform what desperate enterprise I will?
I'll have them fly to Indiá for gold,
Ransack the oceán for orient pearl,
And search all corners of the new-found world
For pleasant fruits and princely delicates;
I'll have them read me strange philosophy
And tell the secrets of all foreign kings. . . .
I'll have them fill the public schools with silk,
Wherewith the students shall be bravely clad;
I'll levy soldiers with the coin they bring,
And chase the Prince of Parma from our land,
And reign sole king of all the provinces.
—CHRISTOPHER MARLOWE, *Doctor Faustus*

CHAPTER 6

Sacred and Philosophic Paraphrase

THE secular ambitions and the philosophic ideals of Bacon, each at times gainsaying the other, could but lead to contradictions in his life. Because of these contradictions, we remember Bacon as a man who is like every other man: he was driven in one direction by the desire for action, which leads to mere worldly success; but he was driven also in the opposite direction by the desire for reflection, which leads to the well-being and spiritual progress of all men. The two drives are but the urges of the body and the urges of the soul.

The writings of Bacon are analogous to the life of Bacon. His letters, multitudinous and varied, are generally self-seeking pleas which require little close attention. His apologies, with their tendency to justify actions demanded by the practices of the age, merit only the comment that they tend to clear him of the condemnation awarded him by injudicious minds. His biographies, although significant historically, were written to please royalty and are not intrinsically attractive; they can, therefore, be passed over rapidly. Likewise, he produced many other works to justify himself as an attorney, judge, and adviser to the king which require little or no space even though they attest the versatility of interest of the author. Such works include *An Advertisement Touching An Holy War, The Arguments of the Law, The Beginning of the History of Great Britain, Certain Articles or Considerations Touching the Union of the Kingdoms of England and Scotland, Certain Considerations Touching the Better Pacification and Edification of the Church of England, The Jurisdiction of the Marches, The Learned Reading . . . upon the Statute of Uses, Maxims of the Law, A Preparation toward the Union of Laws, Transportata, Of the True Greatness of . . . Britain,* and others less well-known.

In his collections of thoughts of others, in his reflections upon those thoughts, and in his writings on them we find the real and immortal Bacon. Discussion of the major works which fall into logical groups requires violation of chronology; such violation further justifies itself by the fact that many of his works were not published until after his death.

I *Religious Writer*

May "God the Father, God the Word, God the Spirit" open "to us new refreshments out of the fountains of his goodness, for the alleviating of our miseries," Bacon says in "The first Prayer, called by his Lordship The Student's Prayer." He then supplicates "the unlocking of the gates of sense, and the kindling of a greater natural light" but not at the expense of "incredulity or intellectual night" toward "the Divine Mysteries." [1] This traditional prayer is included in the *Baconiana* and was published in the Latin of Bacon in the preface to the *Great Restoration*.

The Preface to this work is followed by "The Plan of the Work," an outline closed with "The second Prayer, called by his Lordship The Writer's Prayer." Included also in the *Baconiana*, it invokes the Lord to "protect and govern this work, which coming from thy Goodness returneth to thy Glory." He continues, "Man, reflecting on the works which he had made, saw that *all was vanity and vexation of Spirit*." [2]

"A Confession of Faith" by "Mr. Bacon" was written apparently before 1603 when Bacon became a knight. It is an elaboration and a personalization of the Apostles' Creed as it appears in the second prayer book of Edward VI of 1552 and the prayer book of Elizabeth of 1559; and it is also similar to the Nicene Creed. In the "Confession," Bacon declares his faith in the Trinity, in "an universal or catholic Church of God," and in a life "everlasting without change." God created heaven and earth "and all their armies and generations, and gave unto them constant and everlasting laws, which we call *Nature*, which is nothing but the laws of the creation." Eternity, he says, has three parts: that before the creation, that from the creation to doomsday, and that which is "everlasting without change." The succession of the priesthood he affirms, and he believes Christ to be "a corner-stone to remove the separation between Jew and Gentile." [3]

Meditationes Sacrae, published in 1597 in a volume with the

Sacred and Philosophic Paraphrase

Colours of Good and Evil and with the *Essays*, was composed in Latin because, as Bacon says in a letter to his friend Tobie Matthew, "these modern languages will. . . play the bankrowte with books." In *Religious Meditations* he contents himself with a sensitive retelling of Biblical stories presented in the form of twelve essays, each with an appropriate text. "Of the Works of God and the Works of Man" emphasizes the philosophy that to "labour in God's works" will bring as reward "delightful contemplation," but to follow "the mighty things of men" can bring only "pain and distress" in looking back at one's works. "Of the Miracles of Our Saviour" is stylistically one of the best of the essays, liberally using figurative language, repetition, and balance: "The spirit of Jesus was the spirit of the dove. Those servants of God were as God's oxen. . . . Jesus was the Lamb of God." In the third essay, "Of the Innocency of the Dove and the Wisdom of the Serpent," Bacon urges man to aspire to a "fructifying and begetting goodness" and not to "fear infection or pollution; for the sun entereth into sinks and is not defiled." There are three degrees of charity, he says in "Of the Exaltation of Charity": forgiveness of enemies when they repent; forgiveness of enemies even without offerings of reconciliation; and the bestowal of "pardon and grace" and "favours and benefits." We must not, he says in "Of Moderation of Cares," dwell long on cares; we must "be creatures of to-day . . . not of to-morrow, . . . for to-morrow will have its turn and become today." The sixth essay, "Of Earthly Hope," in addition to the prefixed text, ends in verse: "Long hope to cherish in so short a span/Befits not man." The kernel of this essay is the reflection that "such tranquillity as depends upon hope" is "light and unsure."

"Of Hypocrites," more worldly than the other essays, inevitably brings to mind the more witty essay "The Hypocrite" of Joseph Hall, published eleven years later. Like Hall, Bacon condemns hypocrites who "seek by a pretended holiness towards God to cover their injuries towards men." Bacon, in the next essay, "Of Impostors," says that in their communion with God and man both hypocrites and impostors conduct themselves like inspired men, but that in solitude they are cold and "full of malice and leaven." A facile transition is made from "Of Impostors" to "Of the Kinds of Imposture," an essay masterful in structure: a triple text urges man to avoid "novelties of terms, . . . idle fables," and "high speech." He says at the beginning of the essay that there are "three kinds of speech" or "styles of imposture"; he closes the essay with the statement that the first kind "entangles man's sense and understanding, the second allures, the third astonishes: all seduce it."

The tenth essay, "Of Atheism," is based on the text, "The fool hath said in his heart, There is no God," and Bacon gives emphasis in the explication to *fool, said,* and *heart;* in many respects, this essay is like the sixteenth one in the 1625 edition of the *Essays.* "Ignorance of the will, and ignorance or superficial consideration of the power of God," is the theme of the eleventh essay, "Of Heresies." In the last and twelfth essay of *Religious Meditations,* entitled "Of the Church and the Scriptures," Bacon says that outside "the tabernacle of God" one will "find no end of controversies" and that, therefore, one must betake oneself "to the unity of the Church."[4]

A third prayer, found only in the *Remains* edited by an unknown person, is entitled "A Prayer made and used by the late Lord Chancellor." The prayer books of Edward VI and of Elizabeth led Bacon to paraphrase Psalm XIX, 14 and to continue with a prayer much like A General Confession.[5]

Bacon wrote his fourth prayer soon after he had made his will, in which he bequeathed his "soul to God above" and his "name to the next ages, and to foreign nations." The date of the will is April 10, 1621.[6] The prayer of the will is deeply affecting because of the application of the words of the ritual to Bacon himself: "O Lord," he says, "ever as my worldly blessings were exalted, so secret darts from thee have pierced me . . . . And now when I thought most of peace and honour, thy hand is heavy upon me, and hath humbled me, according to thy former loving-kindness . . . . Just are the judgments upon me for my sins." He ends; "My soul hath been a stranger in the course of my pilgrimage. Be merciful unto me (O Lord) for my Saviour's sake, and receive me into thy bosom, or guide me in thy ways."[7]

II *Psalmist and Poet*

Translation and versification of the Psalms was a fashion among the upper classes in the age of Elizabeth and James, a fashion that

Sacred and Philosophic Paraphrase

originated in *Certain Psalms,* published by Thomas Sternhold in 1548. King James, finding a precedent in the *Scots Psalter* of 1564, with the aid of Sir William Alexander engaged in 1620 in the translation of the Psalms. Bacon followed the path of his family, many of whom had translated religious works, and of the king in turning some of the Psalms into modern English. He calls *Translation of Certaine Psalmes into English Verse,* published in 1625, "this poor exercise of my sickness."[8] Appropriately, he dedicated the work to George Herbert, clergyman and poet, "in respect of divinity and poesy met."

Bacon versified only seven Psalms: 1, 12, 90, 104, 126, 137, and 149. The meter is mechanical; the foot iambic, often arbitrarily so; and the rhyme scheme simple. In Psalms 90, 137, and 149 he uses a pentametric quatrain rhyming *abab* followed by an heroic couplet; in Psalm 1 he uses tetrametric verse and in 12 pentametric verse, both rhyming *ababcdcd;* and in 104 he uses the heroic couplet. The opening couplet of 104 reveals common poetic weaknesses, *viz.,* faulty accent; elision, the weapon of defense of the unskilled poet; and the inappropriate word for the sake of rhyme: "FATHER and king of *pow'rs,* both high and low,/Whose sounding fame all creatures serve to *blow*." A longer sample is the fifth stanza of Psalm 90:

> Thou buriest not within oblivion's tomb
> Our trespasses, but ent'rest them aright;
> Ev'n those that are conceiv'd in darkness' womb
> To thee appear as done at broad day-light.
> As a tale told, which sometimes men attend,
> And sometimes not, our life steals to an end.

A philosphical poem beginning "The man of life upright" is attributed to Bacon in two manuscripts, but it is more probably the work of Thomas Campion.[9] But another philosophical poem can be ascribed to Bacon with a degree of certainty. In 1629, three years after Bacon's death, Thomas Farnaby published a collection of Greek epigrams with the title in Greek, *The Anthology of the Anthology,* and with a subtitle in Latin, *Florilegium Epigrammatum Graecorum;* in it an epigram in Greek by Poseidippus is included. On the opposite page appears a Latin translation, after which it is stated that the elegant imitation of Lord Verulam follows. Farnaby's work was republished in 1650 and again in 1671. Bacon's poem, found among the papers of Sir Henry Wotton, was printed in *Reliquiae Wottonianae*, 1651; ten years later it was included in *Merry Drollery*. The Greek epigram follows:

> Ποίην τις βιότοιο τάμοι τρίβον; εἰν ἀγορῇ μὲν
> Νείκεα καὶ χαλεπαὶ πρήξιες · ἐν δὲ δόμοις
> Φροντίδες · ἐν δ' ἀγροῖς καμάτων ἅλις · ἐν δὲ θαλάσσῃ
> Τάρβος · ἐπὶ ξείνης δ', ἢν μὲν ἔχῃς τι, δέος ·
> Ἢν δ' ἀπορῇς, ἀνιηρόν. ἔχεις γάμον; οὐκ ἀμέριμνος
> Ἔσσεαι · οὐ γαμέεις; ζῇς ἔτ' ἐρημότερος.
> Τέκνα πόνοι · πήρωσις ἄπαις βίος · αἱ νεότητες
> Ἄφρονες · αἱ πολιαὶ δ' ἔμπαλιν ἀδρανέες.
> Ἢν ἄρα τοῖνδε δυοῖν ἑνὸς αἵρεσις, ἢ τὸ γενέσθαι
> Μηδέποτ', ἢ τὸ θανεῖν αὐτίκα τικτόμενον.[10]

The epigram has been translated into English verse:

> What life shall a man choose? In court and mart
> Are quarrels and hard dealing; cares at home;
> Labours by land; terrors at sea; abroad,
> Either the fear of losing what thou hast,
> Or worse, nought left to lose; if wedded, much
> Discomfort; comfortless unwed; a life
> With children troubled, incomplete without;
> Youth foolish, age outworn. Of these two choose then:
> Or never to be born, or straight to die.[11]

Bacon's expanded poem follows:

> The world's a bubble, and the life of man
>   less than a span;
> In his conception wretched, from the womb
>   so to the tomb:
> Curst from the cradle, and brought up to years
>   with cares and fears.
> Who then to frail mortality shall trust,
> But limns the water, or but writes in dust.
>
> Yet since with sorrow here we live opprest,
>   what life is best?

Sacred and Philosophic Paraphrase

> Courts are but only superficial schools
>   to dandle fools.
> The rural parts are turned into a den
>   of savage men.
> And where's the city from all vice so free,
> But may be term'd the worst of all the three?
>
> Domestic cares afflict the husband's bed,
>   or pains his head.
> Those that live single take it for a curse,
>   or do things worse.
> Some would have children; those that have them moan,
>   or wish them gone.
> What is it then to have or have no wife,
> But single thraldom, or a double strife?
>
> Our own affections still at home to please
>   is a disease:
> To cross the seas to any foreign soil
>   perils and toil.
> Wars with their noise affright us: when they cease,
>   we are worse in peace.
> What then remains, but that we still should cry
> Not to be born, or being born to die.[12]

The compactness of the epigram gives it virility. Bacon's expanded paraphrase unmans the epigram; and although the closeness of rhyme, as in "the life of man/less than a span," lends a plaintive quality to the poem, more frequently the proximity creates insipidity, as in "take it for a curse,/or do things worse."

III *Of Poesy and Poets*

Bacon said many things of poetry and poets, some of which will be later considered. "Poesy is as a dream of learning," he says in the *Advancement of Learning*, "a thing sweet and varied, and that would be thought to have in it something divine."[13] In the seventh book of the translation of *De Augmentis Scientiarum* he quotes St. Augustine as having said that poetry is "the wine of demons" because it "engenders temptations, desires, and vain opinions."[14] In *Apophthegms* he quotes Sir Henry Savill: poets are "the best writers, next to those that write prose."[15]

But it is in the close of a letter dated March 28, 1603, to John Davies, fellow attorney and poet, that Bacon roused his idolaters "in foreign nations, and the next ages." "Be good," he says to Davies, "to concealed poets." [16] No one knows how to interpret Bacon's letter. Davies had "then gone to the King, at his first entrance," and Bacon told Davies, "I am not asleep." He urged the performing of "all the good offices which the vivacity of your wit can suggest" and the "well using of my name." *Concealed* causes no difficulty because Bacon was concealed from the king, who saw Bacon only through Davies. Bacon being a Greek scholar and the infinitive ποιέω meaning do, make, or accomplish—may have meant by *poets* simply doers, makers, or accomplishers—the two words together meaning secreted workers. Or it may be that Bacon had written for Essex poetry for various occasions, just as he had prepared masques for presentation by Essex.

The phrase "concealed poets" gave to the Baconians some of the ammunition they needed in a vain attempt to prove that Bacon wrote not only all the works attributed to Shakespeare but that he translated the King James version of the Bible and composed all the plays of Lope de Vega, born a year after Bacon. A rapid comparison of Bacon's verse and Shakespeare's sonnets instantly convinces the reader that the two men were quite different. Nor could Bacon have written the plays of Shakespeare, even conceding that he did write some masques. Valid contemporary evidence, like that of Ben Jonson who wrote of both men, is overwhelming as to each man's operating in his own sphere. But Bacon is the best authority regarding his talent in verse. In his *Apology* concerning Essex, he says: "Her Majesty had a purpose to dine at my lodge at Twicknam Park, at which time I had (though I profess not to be a poet) prepared a sonnet directly tending and alluding to draw on her Majesty's reconcilement to my Lord." [17]

CHAPTER 7

Playmaker

SOME of Bacon's writings, like the *New Atlantis*, are highly dramatic in places, but a contradiction in his personality and in his literary taste lies in apparently serious contribution to the drama. He explains his interest in his essay "Of Masques and Triumphs," numbered XXXVII in the 1625 edition of the *Essays*. The masque in Bacon's day was a dramatic spectacle in which gods or wise men or virtues were personified and associated with a contemporary monarch or other distinguished person; a triumph was a pageant. Bacon begins his essay: "THESE things are but toys, to come amongst such serious observations. But yet, since princes will have such things, it is better they should be graced with elegancy than daubed with cost." And he closes the essay, "But enough of these toys."

Bacon's principal interest obviously was to please royalty and nobility. In the same essay he recognized the fondness of King James for the antimasque: "Let antimasques not be long; they have been commonly of fools, satyrs, baboons, wild-men, antics, beasts, sprites, witches, Ethiops, pigmies, turquets [Turks], nymphs, rustics, Cupids, statua's moving, and the like." But there was a subordinate reason for Bacon's interest in the masque: to confirm the reputation of the Inns of Court as nurseries of the drama and to cement the friendship between the Inns of Court and royalty and nobility.

I *A Hand in a Drama and a Triumph*

"I trust they will not mum nor mask nor sinfully revel at Gray's Inn," Lady Bacon wrote to her son Anthony three weeks before Christmas of 1594. "Who were sometime counted first, God grant they wane not daily and deserve to be named last."[1] Lady Bacon's puritanical prayer was too late: Francis in 1588 had joined

Thomas Hughes and seven other members of Gray's Inn in writing and producing *The Misfortunes of Arthur*, an important play because it is the first English drama to use the Arthurian legend and the first to combine Senecan tragedy and English myth. The atmosphere of a law court is created in a preliminary masque. In the use of a ghost, nymphs, dumb shows, a messenger, and a chorus, *The Misfortunes of Arthur* follows the conventions of Classical tragedy. Bacon, aided by John Lancaster and Christopher Yelverton, wrote the dumb shows.[2]

Bacon also wrote the dialogue for a spectacular with which the Earl of Essex entertained Queen Elizabeth on November 17, 1592. The manuscript bears the title, "Mr. Fr: Bacon of tribute or giving that wch is due." As in John Heywood's interlude *The Playe Called the Four PP.*, four persons engage in the discussion. The first praises the worthiest virtue, fortitude; the second, the worthiest affection, love; the third, the worthiest power, knowledge; the fourth, the worthiest person, Elizabeth herself.[3]

II Gesta Grayorum

Even while Lady Bacon was fretting about the sinfulness of masques and worrying because Anthony had moved to the neighborhood of the Bull Inn, where plays and interludes were acted, Francis was contributing to a masque:

> Gesta Grayorum: OR, THE HISTORY Of the High and Mighty Prince, Henry Prince of Purpoole, Arch-Duke of Stapulia and Bernardia, Duke of High and Nether Holborn, Marquis of St. Giles and Tottenham, Count Palatine of Bloomsbury and Clerkenwell, Great Lord of the Cantons of Islington, Kentish-Town, Paddington and Knightsbridge, Knight of the most Heroical Order of the Helmet, and Sovereign of the Same; Who Reigned and Died, A. D. 1594.[4]

The law students at Gray's Inn decided to devote the twelve days of the Christmas celebration to conversion of the law school into a royal court. They elected a prince, the Prince of Purpoole or Portpool, an early name of the area in which Gray's stood; and they gave him a chamber for audiences and another for council meetings. They then formally invited the gentlemen of the Inner Temple to attend their first celebration on December 20. The ambassador of Frederick Templarius, sovereign of the Inner Temple,

Playmaker

made his grand entrance on December 28; but he was accompanied by such a cortege of lords and ladies who cluttered the stage that the show planned for the ambassador could not be given. Instead, after dancing and general revelry, "a *Comedy of Errors* (like to Plautus his Menechmus)" was acted. Thereafter the night of December 28 was called "the *Night of Errors.*" The gentlemen of Gray's, endeavoring to conceal their chagrin, ordered His Highness' council to investigate the errors. On the next night it was charged that a sorcerer erected scaffolds and invited guests to a play but foisted upon the audience common fellows to create disorder with a play of errors and confusions. In a brilliant burlesque of criminal procedure, the law students acquitted the prisoner at the bar but imprisoned the attorney and the solicitor in the Tower of London.

Gesta Grayorum was continued through the Christmas season and into the new year. Several members of the privy council, the lord keeper, and the lord treasurer attended on January 3, 1595. After the ambassador from the Inner Temple and his retinue were seated next to the Prince of Purpoole, the performance began with a dumb show. Nymphs and fairies sang before the Goddess of Amity, who was to reconcile the two law schools. Then, in pairs appeared Classical friends, Achilles and Patroclus, and Pylades and Orestes, and others, with Graius and Templarius appearing last. The ambassador from the Inner Temple and twenty-four of his retinue received the Collar of the Knighthood of the Helmet—gentle satire of the Order of the Garter—and each swore to uphold the articles of the order; among others, they were never to say that "his Highness' sports were well sorted with a Play of Errors"; never to procure from "his Highness to any widow or maid, for his enablement or commendation to be advanced in marriage." They were always "to perform all requisite and manly service, be it night-service or otherwise, as the case requireth, to all ladies and gentlewomen, beautiful by nature or by art"; always to wear three colors for each mistress; and always "to yield all homage, loyalty, unaffected admiration, and all humble service to the incomparable Empress of the fortunate Island." [5]

To say with certainty that Bacon created the general plan of *Gesta Grayorum,* or that he aided in the creation of it, is impossible. But that he wrote the concluding speeches of the revel is, mainly on the basis of internal evidence, certain. After the investiture of the Knights of the Helmet and after a concert followed by a banquet, six lords of the privy council of the Prince of Purpoole were placed at a table in front of the throne; and each was asked, in turn, to advise the prince of the ways in which he might improve his state. The first urges the exercise of warfare; the second, the study of philosophy; the third, the achievement of fame by buildings and foundations; the fourth, absoluteness of state and treasure; the fifth, the pursuit of virtue and the creation of a gracious government; and the sixth, the seeking of health in pastimes and sports. The prince exhorts the members of his council to accept and act upon the advice of the last speaker. The attribution of the speeches to Bacon by James Spedding is positive: "That the speeches of the six councillors were written by him, and by him alone, no one . . . will for a moment doubt. They carry his signature in every sentence. . . . All these councillors speak with Bacon's tongue and out of Bacon's brain; but the second and fifth speak out of his heart and judgment also." [6]

The achievements of the Prince of Purpoole were lauded until Shrove Tuesday. The law students of Gray's Inn, as late as February 2, 1618, performed the tilt of the Prince of Purpoole and ended with a song in honor of the lord chancellor, Sir Francis Bacon.[7]

III A Device for Elizabeth and Essex

Toward the end of the same year, 1595, an incident that caused embarrassment to both Queen Elizabeth and Essex inspired Bacon to write another device: when a book published in Holland on the succession to the throne, and dedicated to Essex because he would have greatest influence in determining the succession, reached the queen, she showed it to Essex on November 3. He became melancholic and the queen, with characteristic perverseness, attempted to exorcise his dark spirits by turning over to him for reply some important state correspondence. To show his thanks, Essex entertained Elizabeth on Queen's Day, November 17, with a device written by Bacon. The principal character is Erophilus, or Lover of Love, the Earl of Essex. Philautia, Self-love or the Melancholy Essex, endeavors to persuade Erophilus to resist his affection for the queen and to pursue his own happiness.

Playmaker

An account of the masque, written five days after it was presented, says that when Essex appeared he was met by a hermit, who "presented him with a book of meditations"; a secretary of state, who presented him "with political discourses"; a brave soldier, who delivered "orations of brave-fought battles"; and "his own follower, to whom the other three imparted much of their purpose," the fourth role being played by Bacon's closest friend, Tobie Matthew. "In the after-supper, before the Queen," the account continues, each of the counselors advised Essex to take the path of life which he had followed. But because those who had seen the masque began to compare "the Hermit and the Secretary to two of the lords, and the Soldier to Sir Roger Williams, . . . the Queen said that if she had thought there had been so much said of her, she would not have been there that night, and so went to bed." [8]

The speeches as they were delivered were undoubtedly written by Bacon but have an order different from that presented in the contemporary account. The squire, speaking in the tiltyard, beseeches the "most excellent and most glorious Queen" to free his master, "tormented with the importunity of a melancholy dreaming Hermit, a mutinous brain-sick Soldier, and a busy tedious Secretary," from all trouble except "care how to please and honour you." Each of the other players urges that the queen permit Erophilus or Essex to follow his philosophy. The hermit petitions that he "offer his service to the Muses" and "embrace the life of study and contemplation." The soldier, convinced that Essex "had rather be a falcon, a bird of prey, than a singing-bird in a cage," says: "It is the wars that giveth all spirits of valour not only honour but contentment," and all the virtues, wisdom, justice, temperance, fortitude, and constancy. The statesman, however, thinks that "contemplation is a dream, love a trance, and the humour of war is raving." His "advice to thy master shall be as a token wrapped up in words; but then will it show itself fair, when it is unfolded in his actions." "Let policy and matter of state," he argues, "be the chief, and almost the only thing he intends. . . . And ever rather let him take the side which is likeliest to be followed, than that which is soundest and best, that everything may seem to be carried by his direction."

"Wandering Hermit, storming Soldier, and hollow Statesman,"

[61]

the squire replies in a bravura passage, "the enchanting orators of Philautia, which have attempted by your high charms to turn resolved Erophilus into a status deprived of action, or into a vulture attending about dead bodies, or into a monster with a double heart, . . . will you compare shadows with bodies, picture with life, variety of many beauties with the peerless excellency of one? the element of water with the element of fire?" Turning to the statesman, he says, "Untrue Politique, . . . your life is nothing but a continual acting upon a stage; . . . your outward person must serve your end; so as you carry in one person two several servitudes to contrary masters." The masque ends with the resolution of Erophilus: "he renounceth Philautia, and all her enchantments. For her recreation, he will confer with his muse; for her defence and honour, he will sacrifice his life in the wars . . .; to her service will he consecrate all his watchful endeavours; and will ever bear in his heart the picture of her beauty, in his actions of her will, and in his fortune of her grace and favour." [9]

IV The Marriage of the Thames and the Rhine

The marriage of Princess Elizabeth, daughter of King James, to the Count Palatine of the Rhine, strengthened Protestantism in all Europe and occasioned revelry throughout England and especially at the Inns of Court. On February 15, 1613, the day after the wedding, the gentlemen of the Middle Temple and Lincoln's Inn celebrated the wedding with *The Masque of the Middle Temple and Lincoln's Inn,* composed by George Chapman and staged by Inigo Jones. Not to be outclassed, the rival Inns of Court decided to present on February 16, 1613, *The Masque of the Inner-Temple and Gray's Inn* or *The Marriage of the Thames and the Rhine,* composed by Francis Beaumont, a member of the Inner Temple. The masque is dedicated to Francis Bacon:

Ye that spared no time nor travail in the setting forth, ordering and furnishing of this Masque (being the first fruits of honour in this kind which these two Societies have offered to his majesty) will not think much now to look back upon the effects of your own care and work; for that, whereof the success was then doubtful, is now happily performed and graciously accepted; and that which you were then to think of in straits of time, you may now peruse at leisure: and you, Sir Francis Bacon, especially, as you did then by your countenance

Playmaker

and loving affection advance it, so let your good word grace it and defend it, which is able to add value to the greatest and least matters.

The gentlemen of the Middle Temple and Lincoln's Inn having traveled to Whitehall on horseback, those of the Inner Temple and Gray's Inn decided upon a procession by water. The decision appeared to be appropriate in that Gray's Inn had in 1595 presented *The Masque of Proteus*, in which the Thames appeared as one of the characters; moreover, the myth of the wedding of Tethys and Oceanus had been revived by Spenser in *The Faerie Queene* (IV, xi) and was fresh in the mind of every one. Accordingly, on February 16, the gentlemen embarked in galleys and barges, ornate in decoration and illumination, preceded by two admirals. Music resounded throughout the voyage, and three ordnance salutes thundered at embarkation and at debarkation at Whitehall. The royal family reviewed the procession from a gallery. But the gentlemen could not perform their masque on February 16:

The Hall was so full that it was not possible to avoid it, or make room for them. . . . But the worst of all was, that the King was so wearied and sleepy with sitting up almost two whole nights before, that he had no edge to it. Whereupon Sir Francis Bacon ventured to entreat his Majesty, that by this disgrace he would not as it were bury them quick; and I hear the King should answer, that they must bury him quick, for he could last no longer; but withal gave them very good words, and appointed them to come again on Saturday. But the grace of the masque is quite gone, when their apparel hath been already showed, and their devices vented.[10]

But on Saturday, February 20, 1613, the gentlemen played their masque with great enthusiasm. Mercury and Iris, representing Jupiter and Juno, open the play with tribute to the Thames and the Rhine. Four naiads rise from fountains in the first antimasque and engage in a dance; the five Hyades then descend from a cloud, emblematic of the feeding of rivers by springs and showers; four Cupids then appear in flame-colored taffeta; and four statues in gold and silver. Iris, who thinks this antimasque quite ornate, commands her companion, Flora, to introduce a country dance; and the characters of the second antimasque swarm in: pedant,

May-lord, May-lady, servingman, chambermaid, country clown, country wench, host, hostess, he-baboon, she-baboon, he-fool, and she-fool. King James was so much pleased that he requested that the antimasques be repeated, but they could not be given again because one of the statues had undressed. Mercury, in the main masque, revived the Olympian games by presenting fifteen Olympian knights accompanied by twelve priests. Following dancing, the priests sang the concluding song:

> Peace and silence be the guide
> To the man, and to the bride!
> If there be a joy yet new
> In marriage, let it fall on you,
>   That all the world may wonder!
> If we should stay, we should do worse,
> And turn our blessing to a curse,
>   By keeping you asunder.

Sir Edward Phelips wrote to Sir Dudley Carleton on February 25 that "never Kinge was more gloriously and royally served by them, nor they more honoured or graced by a souvraigne."[11]

V The Masque of Flowers

Bacon bore the entire cost of presenting a masque at Whitehall on Twelfth Night, January 6, 1614, called *The Masque of Flowers*. The masque—written by three unidentified persons with the initials J.G., W.D., and T.B.—was presented by the gentlemen of Gray's Inn in the presence of James I to celebrate the marriage of his favorite, Robert Carr, Earl of Somerset, to the divorced wife of the Earl of Essex. The dedication, probably written by the three authors, is "To the Very Honourable Knight, Sir Francis Bacon, His Majesty's Attorney-General," the "only person that did both encourage and warrant the gentlemen to shew their good affection towards so noble conjunction in a time of such magnificence."

At the opening of *The Masque of Flowers*, Invierno or Winter, an aged man covered with icicles and snow engages in dialogue with Primavera or Spring, who is femininely beautiful in an adornment of flowers. The Sun commands the two seasons to entertain the bridal couple. Then Silenus, friend of Bacchus, and Kawasha, imported from Virginia, begin the first antimasque with

Playmaker

competition in song and dance. Silenus in a strophe praises his can of wine and Kawasha in an antistrophe his "men of ire" who are "snuffing, puffing, smoke, and fire." The followers of Silenus and those of Kawasha dance the second antimasque; the former are represented by courtesan, usurer, midwife, and others; the latter, by bawd, mountebank, chimney sweep, and others. A luxuriant garden appears with the drawing of a curtain: in it are a golden Neptune, spouting water from his mouth; and thirteen men, transformed from flowers and garbed in white satin doublets in the shape of lilies. The young men dance informally with the ladies, and the masque ends with tribute to the newly married couple:

> Lovely couple, Seasons two
> Have performed what they can do;
> If the gods inspire our song,
> The other two will not stay long.
> Receive our Flowers with gracious hand,
> As a small wreath to your garland;
> Flowers of honour, Flowers of beauty
>   Are your own; we only bring
> Flowers of affection, Flowers of duty.

The king, the queen, and the prince each extended a hand for kissing by each of the masquers, who were then entertained at a royal banquet.[12]

"But," Bacon says in his *De Augmentis Scientiarum*, "we stay too long in the theatre; let us now pass to the palace of the mind, which we are to approach and enter with more reverence and attention."

CHAPTER 8

From Chrysalis to Essays

TO Francis Bacon, memorabilia were not complete unless they were recorded. He did not trust his excellent memory but faithfully set down in commonplace books the passages that had impressed him in his extensive reading and the ideas that had occurred to him in his profound thinking. He kept copies of his own letters and of those that he had drafted for others, and he grouped much that he had gathered from his reading in such manner that he might use it with facility and charm in his speeches and writings. Like Aristotle, even in preparing for his literary work, Bacon was a collector and an arranger. These were the materials which he transmuted into the *Essays*. Many of the sententious sayings that he had collected he used not only in the *Essays* but also in later works; and some of the materials that he had used in other works he used in later editions of the *Essays*. To Bacon a thricetold tale, if improved or placed more appropriately in its setting, was not only unobjectionable but desirable.

I *The Larvae in the Letters*

Bacon, at times, acted as the secretary to Essex. In this capacity he put in final form the ideas of Essex; he also composed letters for the signature of Essex. In the letters from which ideas in the *Essays* and other works developed, it is difficult to determine whether the adages are those of Essex or of Bacon, but their relationship to the known writings of Bacon is unmistakable.

A letter written in January, 1596, and signed "E." for "Essex" was addressed to Roger Manners, fifth Earl of Rutland and son-in-law of Sir Philip Sidney, who was preparing to go overseas.[1] "Your Lordship," the letter says, "shall see the beauty of many cities, know the manners of the people of many countries, and learn the language of many nations. Some of these may serve for

From Chrysalis to Essays

ornaments, and all of them for delights." Similarly Bacon's "Of Studies" opens, "Studies serve for delight, for ornament, and for ability." The Earl of Rutland is exhorted not to be "too desirous to contradict," anticipating Bacon's injunction in the same essay, "Read not to contradict." The earl, the letter says, must guard against "believing all you hear," just as Bacon admonishes not to "believe and take for granted." The letter of advice says that one must not "too much prize life which we cannot keep, nor fear death, which we cannot shun," just as Bacon says in "Of Death": "It is as natural to die as to be born." Rutland is told, "The gifts or excellencies of the mind are the same as those are of the body: Beauty, Health, and Strength," and Bacon says in the second book of the *Advancement of Learning* that the good of the body lies in "*health, beauty, strength,* and *pleasure*" and that the mind must be sound, beautiful, strong, and agile.[2] But a few of the many parallels must suffice to illustrate the kinship between elements of the letter and the passages in the known works of Bacon.

A second letter, seemingly a sequal to the first, is addressed "My good Lord" but the signature has been torn off.[3] A few quotations from this letter and from Bacon's essay "Of Travel" reflect the close kinship between the two. The addressee of the letter is to store reflections "not only in your memory" but "rather in good writings and books of account"; in the essay Bacon directs, "Let diaries therefore be brought in use." In the letter the "estates of their princes" and the "courts of justice" must be observed; and, in the essay, "the courts of princes" and the "courts of justice." The visitor is urged in the letter to avoid "your own countrymen" and to "seek acquaintance of the best sort of strangers"; in the essay, he should "sequester himself from the company of his countrymen," associate with "good company of the nation where he travelleth," and "procure recommendation to some person of quality residing in the place whither he removeth."

A third letter, in which the salutation is "My Lord" and the signature "Essex," completes the series.[4] The second paragraph begins: "My first letter to your Lordship did contain generalities: my second was particular to direct you in course of study, and this shall only tell you what are the notes I could wish you to gather in your travel." For the collection, "I had rather you trusted your note-book than your memory," which parallels the directive in

[67]

"Of Travel": "Let him keep also a diary." In the letter the following must be studied: "what ports it hath, what shipping; . . . how their people are armed and trained; what fortified towns and castles; what enemies; what arsenals." In "Of Travel," the following must be observed: "the walls and fortifications of cities and towns, and so the havens and harbours; . . . shipping and navies; . . . armories; arsenals; magazines; . . . training of soldiers."

Although the style of the three letters is very much like that of Bacon, the composition of them cannot be ascribed with certainty to him; and similarities between elements of the letters and elements of the writings of Bacon may indicate merely that Essex and Bacon drew from a common intellectual stockpile. But, even assuming that Essex wrote the letters, they show an intimate mental rapport between Essex and Bacon.

II The Promus of Formularies and Elegancies

In the second book of the *Advancement of Learning*, Bacon recommends the collection of *antitheta* and *formulae*, which he defines as follows:

Antitheta are Theses argued *pro et contra;* wherein men may be more large and laborious; but (in such as are able to do it) to avoid prolixity of entry, I wish the seeds of the several arguments to be cast up into some brief and acute sentences; not to be cited, but to be as skeins or bottoms of thread, to be unwinded at large when they come to be used; supplying authorities and examples by reference. . . .

Formulae are but decent and apt passages or conveyances of speech, which may serve indifferently for differing subjects; as of preface, conclusion, digression, transition, excusation, &c. For as in buildings there is great pleasure and use in the well-casting of the stair-cases, entries, doors, windows, and the like; so in speech, the conveyances and passages are of special ornament and effect.[5]

Bacon had begun a collection such as he recommends as early as December 5, 1594, or even earlier; and he had continued it for at least two years. The product, consisting of fifty folios and containing 1,680 extracts from the works of 328 known authors of the fifteenth, sixteenth, and seventeenth centuries, is in the British Museum. It is called *The Promus of Formularies and Elegancies*

From Chrysalis to Essays

because one of the papers (folio 114) is headed "Formularies, Promus. 27 Jan. 1595," and on the back appear the words "fragments of Elegancyes." [6]

The *Promus* is a commonplace book containing graceful introductions, transitional words and phrases, epistolary closes, courtly compliments, aphorisms, and original thoughts.

The *Promus* is a garner of words, phrases, axioms, and ideas collected because of charm of expression, as aids to composition and later study, and as stimuli to reflection. The material, often set down from memory and sometimes altered to fit into a given context or arranged according to relationship of ideas, consists of extracts from the work of the ancients, including Seneca, Horace, Virgil, and Ovid; from Spanish, Italian, French, and English adages; from John Heywood's *Epigrams,* William Camden's *Remains,* and Erasmus' *Adagia;* and from the Bible. Some of the quotations are sequential; others do not follow the order of the original for an extract from the latter part of a source may precede that of an earlier part.

Many of the extracts appear in the works of so many others that it is difficult to determine the exact source used by Bacon. The following, for instance, appear in both Heywood and Camden:

    473. He must needes swymme that is held up by the chynne.
    637. Let them that be a'cold blowe at the coal.
    954. Better be envyed than pitied.
    963. Better sit still than rise and fall.
    639. The catt would eat fish but she will not wett her foote.
        (This axiom is referred to in *Macbeth,* I, VII:
            Letting "I dare not" wait upon "I would,"
            Like the poor cat i' the adage.)
    840. To looke a gyven horse in the mouthe.
        (Erasmus uses this axiom: *Equi dentes inspicere donati.*
        [To look at a gift horse's teeth.])

Shakespeare and Bacon seem sometimes to have used the same source and at other times to have gone to different sources: No. 517 in the *Promus,* "Good wine needes no bush," appears in the epilogue to Shakespeare's *As You Like It;* and No. 949, "All is well that ends well," is approximately the title of one of Shakespeare's plays, but Heywood included this proverb in his collection. No. 477, "All is not gold that glisters," appears in its more usual form in *The Merchant of Venice* (II, 7); but this epigram appeared in French literature as early as 1300 and was used in nearly the same form by Chaucer, John Lydgate, and Nicholas Udall.

From Proverbs XXX, 2, in the Vulgate, Bacon included No. 234: "The glory of God is to conceal a thing, and the glory of man is to find out a thing." No. 341, "So gyve authors their due as you gyve tyme his due which is to discover truth," was used in much the same manner by Bacon in his work "In Praise of Knowledge."

No. 1595, "Nourriture passe nature," has been used in "Of Custom and Education," in altered form: "Nature, nor the engagement of words, are not so forcible as custom." Nos. 267 and 610 are identical, "Di mentira y sagueras verdad," and reappear in "Of Truth": "A mixture of a lie doth ever add pleasure." Other extracts are used in "Of Ceremonies and Respects" and "Of Followers and Friends." The *Promus* contains thoughts on backbiting and charity, and on dissembling and death, chrysalises brought to adult stage in the *Essays*.

In the sixth book of *De Augmentis Scientiarum*, Bacon gives examples of antitheses.[7] Many of the axioms in the *antitheta* appear in the *Essays*:

II. BEAUTY

For	*Against*
Deformed persons commonly take revenge on nature.	Virtue is like a rich stone, best plain set.
Virtue is nothing but inward beauty; beauty nothing but outward virtue.	As a fair garment on a deformed body, such is beauty in a bad man.
Deformed persons seek to rescue themselves from scorn—by malice.	They that are beautiful and they that are affected by beauty are commonly alike light.
Beauty makes virtues shine, and vices blush.	

The first axiom in the "Against" column is the sentence with which Bacon begins the essay "Of Beauty."

From Chrysalis *to* Essays

III. YOUTH

For

First thoughts and young men's counsels have more of divineness.

Old men are wiser for themselves, not so wise for others and for the commonwealth.

Old age, if it could be seen, deforms the mind more than the body.

Old men are afraid of everything, except the Gods.

Against

Youth is the seedbed of repentance.

There is implanted in youth contempt for the authority of age; so every man must grow wise at his own cost.

The counsels to which Time is not called, Time will not ratify.

In old men the Loves are changed into the Graces.

Obviously, the essay "Of Youth and Age" parallels the preceding example of *antitheta*. As in the first adage in the "For" column, Bacon says in the essay that "imaginations" stream into the minds of young men "as it were more divinely." But ideas are sometimes reversed in the essay. The last axiom in the "For" column implies that old men are close to the gods because they are not afraid of them, but the essay says that "young men are admitted nearer to God than old." The last axiom in the "Against" column implies that old men have more grace than young men, but the essay states that there is "better grace in youth than in age."

V. WIFE AND CHILDREN

For

LOVE of his country begins in a man's own house.

A wife and children are a kind of discipline of humanity; whereas unmarried men are harsh and severe.

To be without wife or children is good for a man only when he wants to run away.

He who begets not children, sacrifices to death.

They that are fortunate in other things are commonly unfortunate in their children; lest men should come too near the condition of Gods.

Against

He that has wife and children has given hostages to fortune.

Man generates and has children; God creates and produces works.

The eternity of brutes is in offspring; of men, in fame, good deserts, and institutions.

Domestic considerations commonly overthrow public ones.

Some persons have wished for Priam's fortune, who survived all his children.

[71]

The third apothegm in the "Against" column appears in altered form in "Of Parents and Children": "The perpetuity by generation is common to beasts; but memory, merit and noble works are proper to men." The first axiom in the same column is the opening clause of the essay "Of Marriage and Single Life": "HE that hath wife and children hath given hostages to fortune. . . ." The third axiom in the "For" column is almost duplicated in the same essay: "Unmarried men . . . are light to run away." The second axiom in the "For" column appears in the essay "Of Marriage and Single Life" in the following form: "Certainly wife and children are a kind of discipline of humanity; and single men . . . are more cruel and hardhearted (good to make severe inquisitors)."

XII. LIFE

For

It is absurd to prefer the accidents of life to life itself.

A long course is better than a short one for everything, even for virtue.

Without a good space of life a man can neither finish, nor learn, nor repent.

Against

Philosophers in making such preparations against death make death itself appear more fearful.

Men fear death, as children fear to go into the dark, because they know not what is there.

There is no human passion so weak but if it be a little roused it masters the fear of death.

A man might wish to die, though he were neither brave nor miserable nor wise, merely from weariness of being alive.

The foregoing observations on life in the "Against" column are included in the essay "Of Death." The first appears in the essay: "Certainly the Stoics bestowed too much cost upon death, and by their great preparations made it appear more fearful." The second is less powerful because more verbose: "MEN fear Death, as children fear to go in the dark; and as that natural fear in children is increased with tales, so is the other." The parallel of the third axiom in the essay is: "There is no passion in the mind of man so weak, but it mates and masters the fear of death." The fourth adage appears as follows in the essay: "A man would die, though he were neither valiant nor miserable, only upon a weariness to do the same thing so oft over and over."

From Chrysalis *to* Essays

Further specimens of the innumerable parallels between Bacon's examples of *antitheta* and axioms found in the *Essays* are unnecessary.

III Of the Colors of Good and Evil

Another work makes a transition from *The Promus of Formularies and Elegancies* to the *Essays: Of the Colors of Good and Evil*. In the book published in 1597 the *Essays* appears first, *Meditationes Sacrae* next, and *Of the Colors of Good and Evil* last. The last work seems to have been composed about 1595 or 1596; in Bacon's hand some seventy or eighty "colors" are contained in a collection in the British Museum, but they are incomplete in form. Only ten were published in 1597 with the title page "OF THE COULERS OF GOOD AND EVILL. A FRAGMENT. 1597." A dedication was written, but not published, by Bacon, who said:

> I send you the last part of the best book of Aristotle of Stagira, who (as your Lordship knoweth) goeth for the best author. But . . . the man being a Grecian and of a hasty wit, having hardly a discerning patience, much less a teaching patience, hath so delivered the matter, as I am glad to do the part of a good househen, which without any strangeness will sit upon pheasants' eggs. And yet perchance some that shall compare my lines with Aristotle's lines, will muse by what art, or rather by what revelation, I could draw these conceits out of that place. But I, that should know best, do freely acknowledge that I had my light from him; for where he gave me not matter to perfect, at the least he gave me occasion to invent. . . . I do not find him to deliver and unwrap himself well of that he seemeth to conceive, nor to be a master of his own knowledge. Neither do I for my part also, (though I have brought in a new manner of handling this argument to make it pleasant and lightsome,) pretend so to have overcome the nature of the subject, but that the full understanding and use of it will be somewhat dark, and best pleasing the tastes of such wits as are patient to stay the digesting and soluting unto themselves of that which is sharp and subtile. . . .[8]

Bacon uses the word *color* as it is used today in the law, meaning a representation as better or worse than the reality, a pretense or false appearance of truth. In the introduction to the 1597 edition he says:

[73]

In deliberatives the point is, what is good and what is evil, and of good what is greater, and of evil what is the less.

So that the persuader's labour is to make things appear good or evil, and that in higher or lower degree; which as it may be performed by true and solid reasons, so it may be represented also by colours, popularities, and circumstances, which are of such force, as they sway the ordinary judgment either of a weak man, or of a wise man not fully and considerately attending and pondering the matter. . . . Lastly, to make a true and safe judgment, nothing can be of greater use and defence to the mind, than the discovering and reprehension of these colours, shewing in what cases they hold, and in what they deceive: which as it cannot be done, but out of a very universal knowledge of the nature of things, so being performed, it so cleareth man's judgment and election, as it is the less apt to slide into any error.[9]

One of the ten "colors" follows:

VI.

Cujus privatio bona, malum; cujus privatio mala, bonum. [That which it is good to be rid of is evil; that which it is evil to be rid of is good.] The forms to make it conceived, that that was evil which is changed for the better, are, *He that is in hell thinks there is no other heaven. Satis quercus; Acorns were good till bread was found,* &c. And of the other side, the forms to make it conceived that that was good which was changed for the worse, are, *Bona magis carendo quam fruendo sentimus:* [it is by missing a good thing that we become sensible of it:] *Bona a tergo formosissima: Good things never appear in their full beauty, till they turn their back and be going away,* &c.

The reprehension of this colour is, that the good or evil which is removed, may be esteemed good or evil comparatively, and not positively or simply. So that if the privation be good, it follows not the former condition was evil, but less good: for the flower or blossom is a positive good, although the remove of it to give place to the fruit be a comparative good. So in the tale of Æsop, when the old fainting man in the heat of the day cast down his burthen and called for death, and when death came to know his will with him, said it was for nothing but to help him up with his burthen again: it doth not follow that because death, which was the privation of the burthen, was ill, therefore the burthen was good. And in this part, the ordinary form of *malum necessarium* aptly reprehendeth this colour; for *privatio mali necessarii est mala,* [to be deprived of an evil that is necessary, is evil], and yet that doth not convert the nature of the necessary evil, but it is evil.

From Chrysalis *to* Essays

Again, it cometh sometimes to pass, that there is an equality in the change or privation, and as it were a *dilemma boni* or a *dilemma mali:* so that the corruption of the one good is a generation of the other; *Sorti pater aequus utrique est:* there is good either way: and contrary, the remedy of the one evil is the occasion and commencement of another, as in Scylla and Charybdis.[10]

Twelve "Examples *of the Colours of Good and Evil, both Simple and Comparative*" are given in *De Augmentis Scientiarum*. One, with a fable from Æsop, the most quoted of the ancients in this work, must suffice:

SOPHISM.

7. *That which keeps the matter open, is good; that which leaves no opening for retreat, is bad. For not to be able to retreat is to be in a way powerless; and power is a good.*

Hence Æsop derived the fable of the two frogs, who in a great drought, when water was everywhere failing, consulted together what was to be done. The first said, "Let us leap down into a deep well, since it is not likely that the water will fail there." But the other rejoined, "Yes, but if it chance that the water fail there also, how shall we be able to get up again?" And the ground of this Sophism is, that human actions are so uncertain and subject to such risks, that that appears the best course which has the most passages out of it. To this belong those forms which are in use,—"You will tie your hands and engage yourself," "You will not be free to take what fortune may offer," &c.

ANSWER.

This Sophism deceives, first because in human actions fortune insists that some resolution shall be taken. For, as it was prettily said by some one, "not to resolve is itself to resolve;" so that many times suspension of resolution involves us in more necessities than a resolution would. And it seems to be the same disease of mind which is found in misers, only transferred from the desire of keeping money to the desire of keeping freedom of will and power. For as the miser will enjoy nothing, because he will not diminish his store, so this kind of sceptic will execute nothing, because he will still keep all in his own hands. It deceives secondly, because necessity, and the casting of the die (as they call it), is a spur to the courage; as one says, "Being a match for them in the rest, your necessity makes you superior." [11]

[75]

CHAPTER 9

Essays

TO his friend Lancelot Andrews, Bishop of Winchester, Bacon wrote in 1622: "As for my *Essays*, and some other particulars of that nature, I count them but as the recreations of my other studies, and in that sort purpose to continue them; though I am not ignorant that those kind of writings would, with less pains and embracement (perhaps), yield more lustre and reputation to my name, than those other which I have in hand."[1]

In a dedication to Henry, Prince of Wales, of the second edition of 1612, discarded because of the death of Henry, Bacon defines the word *essay* as "certain brief notes, set down rather significantly than curiously, which I have called *Essays*. The word is late, but the thing is ancient. For Seneca's epistles to Lucilius, if one mark them well, are but *Essays*, that is, dispersed meditations, though conveyed in the form of epistles. . . . They may be as grains of salt, that will rather give you an appetite than offend you with satiety."[2] Bacon undoubtedly had in mind the essays of Montaigne when he said that "the word is late." In saying that "the thing is ancient," he might have included with the epistles of Seneca, Aristotle's "Of Tragedy" and Cicero's "Concerning Friendship."

In the title Bacon has not clung to the earlier meaning of *essay* as an attempt or an effort to do or to make something but has turned to the newer meaning, that given in the rejected dedication to Prince Henry: "brief notes" or "dispersed meditations."

I First Edition

In 1597, the thirty-ninth year of the reign of Queen Elizabeth, a small octavo volume was offered for sale for twenty pence with the title: *Essayes. Religious Meditations. Places of perswasion and disswasion. Seene and allowed. At London, Printed for Hum-*

Essays

frey Hooper, and are to be sold at the blacke Beare in Chauncery Lane. In the title "Religious Meditations" is used for *Meditationes sacrae* and "Places of perswasion and disswasion" for *Of the Colors of Good and Evil.* The dedication, written at Gray's Inn on January 30 of the new "historical" year 1597 (but not the "civil" year, which began on March 25), is "To M. ANTHONY BACON his deare Brother."

LOUING and beloued Brother, I doe nowe like some that haue an Orcharde il neighbored, that gather their fruit before it is ripe, to preuent stealing. These fragments of my conceites were going to print; To labour the staie of them had bin troublesome, and subiect to interpretation; to let them passe had been to adventure the wrong they mought receiue by vntrue Coppies, or by some garnishment, which it mought please any that should set them forth to bestow upon them. Therefore I helde it best discreation to publish them my selfe as they passed long agoe from my pen, without any further disgrace, then the weaknesse of the Author. . . . Only I disliked now to put them out because they will be like the late new halfe-pence, which though the Siluer were good, yet the peeces were small. But since they would not stay with their Master, but would needes trauaile abroad, I haue preferred them to you that are next myself, Dedicating them, such as they are, to our loue, in the depth whereof (I assure you) I sometimes wish your infirmities translated uppon my selfe, that her Maiestie mought haue the seruice of so actiue and able a mind, & I mought be with excuse confined to these contemplations & studies for which I am fittest. . . .[3]

Ten essays appeared in the 1597 edition: (1) *Of studie;* (2) *Of discourse;* (3) *Of Ceremonies and respects;* (4) *Of followers and friends;* (5) *Sutors.* (6) *Of expence.* (7) *Of Regiment of health;* (8) *Of Honour and reputation;* (9) *Of Faction;* and (10) *Of Negociating.*

The 1597 edition of the *Essays* was highly successful. Although the individual essay is unadorned and is little more than a collection of astute observations on the title, the reader rouses himself at the end of the essay and wonders why he has not written on the same subject with such compactness and power and memorability. The first edition again appeared in 1598, 1604, and 1606 with minor alterations; but Bacon had nothing to do with these reprints which demonstrate the popularity of the first edition.

II *Manuscript for a Second Edition*

Even while pirated issues of the first edition proliferated—and because they were appearing—Bacon prepared an enlarged second edition which was not published. No. 5106 of the Harleian manuscripts in the British Museum is a volume containing thirty-four essays with interlinear writing by Bacon. The title indicates that it was prepared between 1607, when Bacon became the solicitor general, and 1612, when he published the second edition: *The writings of Sr Francis Bacon Knt. the Kinge's Sollicitor Generall: in Moralitie, Policie, and Historie.* The order of the essays follows:

1. Of Friendship.
2. Of Wisdom for a Man's Self.
3. Of Nobility.
4. Of Goodness and Goodness of Nature.
5. Of Beauty.
6. Of Seeming Wise.
7. Of Regiment of Health.
8. Of Expences.
9. Of Ambition.
10. Of Ceremonies and Respects.
11. Of Studies.
12. Of Discourse.
13. Of Riches.
14. Of Followers and Friends.
15. Of Suitors.
16. Of Negociating.
17. Of Despatch.
18. Of Deformity.
19. Of Young Men and Age.
20. Of Faction.
21. Of Honour and Reputation.
22. Of Marriage and Single Life.
23. Of Parents and Children.
24. Of Great Place.
25. Of Empire.
26. Of Counsel.
27. Of Atheism.
28. Of Superstition.
29. Of Praise.
30. Of Nature in Men.
31. Of Custom and Education.
32. Of Fortune.
33. Of Death.
34. Of Seditions and Troubles.[4]

All ten of the essays of the first edition are included in the manuscript. Only two of the manuscript essays were not included in the second edition of 1612: No. 21, included in the editions of 1597 and 1625; and No. 34, not published with authority until 1625.

III *Second Edition*

In 1612 John Beale published at London the second edition of "THE ESSAIES OF SIR FRANCIS BACON KNIGHT THE KINGS SOLLICITER GENERALL." Bacon dedicated this edi-

Essays

tion to Sir John Constable, his literary executor who had married Lady Bacon's sister:

To my Loving Brother, Sir IOHN CONSTABLE Knight.
MY last Essaies I dedicated to my deare brother *Master Anthony Bacon, who is with God. Looking amongst my papers this vacation, I found others of the same Nature: which if I my selfe shall not suffer to be lost, it seemeth the World will not; by the often printing of the former. Missing my Brother, I found you next; in respect of bond both of neare alliance, and of straight friendship and societie, and particularly of communication in studies. Wherein I must acknowledge my selfe beholding to you. For as my businesse found rest in my contemplations; so my contemplations euer found rest in your louing conference and iudgement. So wishing you all good, I remaine*
Your louing brother and friend,
FRA. BACON.[5]

The arrangement of the essays of the second edition follows:

THE TABLE.

1. Of Religion.
2. Of Death.
3. Of Goodnes and goodnes of nature.
4. Of Cunning.
5. Of Marriage and single life.
6. Of Parents and Children.
7. Of Nobilitie.
8. Of Great place.
9. Of Empire.
10. Of Counsell.
11. Of Dispatch.
12. Of Loue.
13. Of Friendshippe.
14. Of Atheisme.
15. Of Superstition.
16. Of Wisdome for a Mans selfe.
17. Of Regiment of Health.
18. Of Expences.
19. Of Discourse.
20. Of Seeming wise.
21. Of Riches.
22. Of Ambition.
23. Of Young men and age.
24. Of Beautie.
25. Of Deformitie.
26. Of nature in Men.
27. Of Custome and Education.
28. Of Fortune.
29. Of Studies.
30. Of Ceremonies and respects.
31. Of Sutors.
32. Of Followers.
33. Of Negociating.
34. Of Faction.
35. Of Praise.
36. Of Iudicature.
37. Of vaine glory.
38. Of greatnes of Kingdomes.
39. Of the publike.
40. Of Warre and peace.[6]

Although the table of contents lists forty essays, the collection is concluded with the thirty-eighth, after which appears the word "FINIS."

The 1612 edition of the essays does not include the eighth essay of the 1597 edition, "Of Honour and Reputation," although the essay is included in the manuscript prepared between 1607 and 1612. The thirty-second essay of the 1612 edition, "Of Followers and Friends," follows closely the fourth essay by the same title of the 1597 edition; but in the 1612 edition a separate essay, the thirteenth, "Of Friendship," has been added. In 1618 an Italian translation of the 1612 edition was published in London by Tobie Matthew, close friend of Bacon, apparently with the approval of Bacon. Included is "Of Seditions and Troubles," first published by Bacon in 1625.

IV Third Edition

John Haviland printed for Hanna Barrett and Richard Whitaker in 1625 the third and last authorized edition, to be sold "at the sign of the King's Head, in Paul's Churchyard," with the title *"THE ESSAYES OR COUNSELS, CIVILL AND MORALL, OF FRANCIS LO. VERULAM, VISCOUNT ST. ALBAN. NEWLY ENLARGED."*

To George Villiers, Duke of Buckingham, lord high admiral of England, and favorite of King James, Bacon dedicated the third edition in the hope that he might propitiate Villiers:

EXCELLENT LO.
SALOMON says, *A good name is as a precious ointment;* and I assure myself, such will your Grace's name be with posterity. For your fortune and merit both have been eminent. And you have planted things that are like to last. I do now publish my Essays; which, of all my other works, have been most current; for that, as it seems, they come home to men's business and bosoms. I have enlarged them both in number and weight; so that they are indeed a new work. I thought it therefore agreeable to my affection and obligation to your Grace, to prefix your name before them, both in English and in Latin. For I do conceive that the Latin volume of them (being in the universal language) may last as long as books last. My Instauration I dedicated to the King; my History of Henry the Seventh (which I have now also translated into Latin), and my portions of Natural History, to the

Essays

Prince; and these I dedicate to your Grace; being of the best fruits that by the good encrease which God gives to my pen and labours I could yield. God lead your Grace by the hand.

Your Grace's most obliged and
faithful seruant,
FR. ST. ALBAN.[7]

The "newly enlarged" edition of 1625 contains fifty-eight essays. Of these, twenty are new and include some of the best essays; practically all the others were altered and enlarged. The twenty added are "Of Truth," "Of Revenge," "Of Adversity," "Of Simulation and Dissimulation," "Of Envy," "Of Boldness," "Of Seditions and Troubles," "Of Travel," "Of Delays," "Of Innovations," "Of Suspicion," "Of Plantations," "Of Prophecies," "Of Masks and Triumphs," "Of Usury," "Of Building," "Of Gardens," "Of Honour and Reputation," "Of Anger," and "Of Vicissitude of Things." In 1638, twelve years after the death of Bacon, his former chaplain, Dr. William Rawley, published a Latin translation of the essays.

V Development of the Essays

The essays in the three editions have many of the qualities of their forerunners: the antitheses and the neat introductions, transitions, and conclusions, for example, of *The Promus of Formularies and Elegancies* and the inclination toward the expedient and the separation of good from evil in *Of the Colors of Good and Evil.* A careful comparison of the essays in the first edition and of the same essays in the second and third editions shows no great improvement in the latter. It is true that the later editions sometimes contain illustrations of generalizations of the 1597 edition and that occasionally transitions are better. Sometimes, however, there is a lamentable loss of coherence and power.

In the revision of the first essay of the 1597 edition, "Of Studies," Bacon in the 1612 edition altered the opening clause from "Studies serve for pastimes" to "Studies serve for delight" and the statement that certain books are to be read "but cursorily" to "but not curiously." To the splendid climax at the end of the 1597 edition beginning, "Histories make men wise, poets witty," he tacked on 116 words beginning *"Abeunt studia in mores.* [Studies pass into manners.]" Impedimenta of the wit, he continues, may be cured by proper studies just as diseases of the body may be helped by proper exercise: shooting, the simile continues irrelevantly, is good for the lungs and breast; walking, for the stomach; riding, for the head. If a man's mind wander, let him study mathematics; if he is unable to make distinctions, let him study the schoolmen; if he is unable to find resemblances, let him study law cases. "So every defect of the mind," the essay ends weakly and with dubious truthfulness, "may have a special receit." In the 1625 edition slight amplification and alteration of the second sentence of the 1612 edition appears; an addition has been made of a similitude between natural abilities and natural plants; the triple-distilled wine of the sentence, "Read not to contradict, nor to believe, but to weigh and consider," has been watered down to "Read not to contradict and confute; nor to believe and take for granted; nor to find talk and discourse; but to weigh and consider." Added are the insidious idea that some books may be read by deputy and the discrediting of the schoolmen, "for they are *cymini sectores* [hairsplitters]."

Similarly the fourth essay, "Of Followers and Friends," of the 1597 edition is developed. The statement in that edition that "ill intelligence" sometimes exists "between great personages" is expanded in the 1612 edition: "Likewise glorious followers are full of inconveniency; for they taint business through want of secrecy, and they export honor from a man and make him a return in envy." In the 1625 edition a descriptive clause appears after "glorious followers": "who make themselves as trumpets of the commendation of those they follow." After the completion of the entire sentence, two additional sentences appear in the 1625 edition: "There is a kind of followers likewise which are dangerous, being indeed espials; which inquire the secrets of the house, and bear tales of them to others. Yet such men, many times, are in great favour; for they are officious, and commonly exchange tales." Elaborating the idea that sometimes it is better to take sides with "the more passable, than with the more able," another addition appears: "And besides, to speak truth, in base times active men are of more use than virtuous." The simple balance and antithesis of, "To be governed by one is not good, and to be distracted with many is worse," in the editions of 1597 and 1612 is destroyed through excessive verbiage in the 1625 edition: "To be governed

Essays

(as we call it) by one, is not safe; for it shews softness, and gives a freedom to scandal and disreputation; for those that would not censure or speak ill of a man immediately, will talk more boldly of those that are so great with them, and thereby wound their honour. Yet to be distracted with many is worse; for it makes men to be of the last impression, and full of change."

But there are other essays which are quite different in the various editions. "Of Friendship" did not appear in the 1597 edition; in the 1612 edition it contains some two hundred seventy words and is a masterpiece of simplicity, good taste, and restrained unity; in the 1625 edition, nine times as long, it runs to about twenty-three hundred words and contains many adages in Latin and many references, direct or indirect, to Aristotle, Plutarch, St. James, Cicero, Tacitus, and many other early authors. In both essays the debt to the essays on friendship by Cicero and Montaigne is great, but it is in the 1612 edition that the ideal friendship of both Cicero and Montaigne is emphasized. Only a few words or phrases link Bacon's two quite distinct essays, with identical titles, published in 1612 and 1625. The profound admiration inspired by the opening sentence of the 1612 essay, "There is no greater desert or wilderness than to be without true friends," turns to tedium in the wordy opening sentence of the 1625 essay: "It had been hard for him that spake it to have put more truth and untruth together in few words, than in that speech, *Whosoever is delighted in solitude is either a wild beast or a god.*" (The quotation is from Aristotle).

The tie with the 1612 essay comes later when Bacon says that, without true friends, "the world is but a wilderness," but here the images created by the comparison and contrast of *desert* and *wilderness* have vanished. In the 1612 edition Bacon says that the lives of some people are "perpetually played upon a stage." Battered and belabored, this simple metaphor verbosely closes the 1625 essay: "But to enumerate these things were endless: I have given the rule, where a man cannot fitly play his own part; if he have not a friend, he may quit the stage." This ending must be compared to the vigorous and warm one of the 1612 essay, in which Bacon says of his friend: "I am open hearted to him; I single him from the generality of those with whom I live; I make him a portion of my own wishes." Such an attitude evokes Montaigne, who said of Étienne de la Boétie, "I am his friend because he is he, and I am I."

Friendship glows in the 1612 edition, where Bacon says that it "multiplieth joys and divideth griefs" and "It is friendship when a man can say to himself, 'I love this man without respect of utility.'" But this sentiment has been bartered cheaply in the 1625 edition for the mere "fruits of friendship" and for the insipid idea that, while there is no recipe, except a good friend for opening the heart of a man, one may take "sarza [sarsaparilla] to open the liver, steel to open the spleen, flower of sulphur for the lungs, castoreum for the brain."

The first edition of the essays conforms to the definition of Samuel Johnson of the essay as "an irregular, undigested piece." Each essay is a series of disjunctive musings with little transition, but each thought inspires contemplation by the reader. In the later editions the seams are less visible; but, although the ligatures are good, unlike elements are joined and chronology is ignored. The very compression of each essay in the first edition creates a cold virginity of style and a prophetic quality lacking in the later essays.

The subject of each of the essays of the 1597 edition is abstract, a noun or two nouns used without thought of particular instances or material objects or developed from personal experience. The essays of the second edition are also on abstractions: although Bacon had Tobie Matthew in mind when he wrote "Of Friendship" and although he was married at the time that he published in 1612 "Of Marriage and Single Life," he wrote in general impersonally and not from experience as he did when he, childless, wrote "Of Parents and Children." Nevertheless, some essays reflect his official duties: "Of Great Place," "Of Counsel," "Of Dispatch," "Of Discourse," "Of Ceremonies and Respects," "Of Suitors," "Of Followers," "Of Negotiating," and "Of Faction." And "Of Regiment of Health" recalls Bacon's experiments on his own body.

Abstractions continue to be the subject of many of the new essays in the 1625 edition and include "Of Truth," "Of Revenge," "Of Adversity," and others. Some of them, however, may be associated with actual experiences of the author: "Of Building," with the construction of Verulam House; "Of Gardens," with the plant-

Essays

ing of trees and flowers at Gray's Inn; "Of Plantations," with membership in the company of 659 adventurers who attempted to colonize Virginia; and "Of Masques and Triumphs," with Bacon's own dramatic compositions.

VI Sources of the Essays

The material of the essays was taken from virtually all that Bacon had read or done. His own *Short Notes for Civil Conversation,* composed early but not published until 1648 in the *Remains,* is the base from which Bacon sent aloft the essay "Of Discourse." His own letters and others that he may have written for Essex, *The Promus of Formularies and Elegancies,* and *Of the Colors of Good and Evil* are sources. For the critical essay Bacon turned to Aristotle's "Of Tragedy." Bacon turned, in addition to the Bible and the authors previously mentioned in this chapter, to Herodotus, Homer, Horace, Lucan, Lucian, Lucretius, Ovid, Plato, Plautus, the Plinies, Suetonius, and Virgil. Just as Bacon took from many tongues, just so his essays have been translated into almost every known language.

VII Structure of the Essays

Contrast, balance, similitude, and maxim, and impressive opening, smooth transition, and climactic close impress the reader of the essays. Structurally, the essays are a series of statements intended to confirm or refute an idea; they are presented in judicial manner as are the evidence for the prosecution and that for the defense; but there is no decision by judge or jury; for the reader, to whom compliment is paid by the method, evaluates the evidence and makes up his own mind.

VIII Style of the Essays

Bacon revived many obsolescent words and created a number of new ones. He took old aphorisms and gave them a new setting or slightly altered them to fit his context with the result that he is one of the most quoted of authors. The propriety of the axiom, its antithesis, and its succinctness declare it to be a maxim from Bacon:

Death . . . openeth the gate to good fame and extinguisheth envy.

Revenge is a kind of wild justice.

He that hath wife and children hath given hostages to fortune.

For envy is a gadding passion and walketh the streets.

Nuptial love maketh mankind; friendly love perfecteth it; but wanton love corrupteth and embaseth it.

The French are wiser than they seem, and the Spaniards seem wiser than they are.

Suspicions amongst thoughts are like bats amongst birds: they ever fly by twilight.

God Almighty first planted a garden.

In the essays man sees himself, body and soul, more clearly than in any other literary work—the Bible perhaps excepted.

Although Bacon does not often dematerialize himself and ascend into pure ether as Sir Thomas Browne often does—as when he says, "In vain do individuals hope for immortality. . . . There is nothing strictly immortal but immortality"—Bacon often has some of the impassioned fervor of Browne. Sir Thomas Browne says, "I love to lose myself in a mystery, to pursue my reason to an *O altitudo!*"; and Bacon says in his essay "Of Death": "But see how I am swerved, and lose my course, touching at the soul, that doth least hold action with death, who hath the surest property in this frail act; his style is the end of all flesh, and the beginning of incorruption." Bacon is of the company of Jeremy Taylor, who says that "the young man . . . shines like . . . the image of a rainbow, which hath no substance and whose very imagery and colors are fantastical; and so he dances out the gayety of his youth, and is all the while in a storm," and of Sir Walter Raleigh, who in his famous apostrophe to death says, "O eloquent, just, and mighty Death! . . . thou hast drawn together all the far-stretched greatness, all the pride, cruelty, and ambition of man, and covered it all over with these two narrow words, *Hic iacet,*" and of one even greater, an ancient named Socrates, who faced

Essays

death courageously, even happily: "I go to die, and you to live; but which of us goes to the better lot, is known to none but God." Bacon says of death:

> And since I must needs be dead, I require it may not be done before mine enemies, that I be not stript before I be cold: but before my friends. The night was even now; but that name is lost; it is not now late, but early. Mine eyes begin to discharge their watch, and compound with this fleshy weakness for a time of perpetual rest; and I shall presently be as happy for a few hours, as I had died the first hour I was born.

To the Bible he also went for inspiration, and from it he took the illustration which makes familiar the abstruse doctrines of the early Christians, as well as the allegory which makes the teachings memorable. The words of John, "I am the vine, ye are the branches: He that abideth in me, and I in him, the same bringeth forth much fruit: for without me ye can do nothing," are not unlike those of Bacon in "Of Death" in which he says that man, like the tree, derived his being from the earth and draws his nourishment as does a plant, and "made ripe for death he tends downwards, and is sowed, again in his mother the earth, where he perisheth not, but expects a quickening."

For lucidity, eloquence, inspiration, and nobility, the language of Bacon has achieved immortality.

CHAPTER 10

Apologist

AFTER locking three royal emissaries in his library at Essex House on February 8, 1601, Robert Devereux, Earl of Essex, with three hundred men attempted to raise a following among the citizens of London by crying out loudly that his enemies were attempting to murder him and that the English throne was being sold to the Infanta. The people declared him disloyal and began to collect forces to repel him. Essex managed to return to his home, but he was captured and taken to prison. On February 20 he was arraigned. Edward Coke, the attorney general, blundered in the prosecution. Bacon, holding minor legal office by royal command, then took over as a member of the prosecution; vigorously he implored Essex not to justify but to confess. Found guilty, Essex, a short time before his execution in the Tower of London, condemned himself as "the greatest, the most vilest, and most unthankful traitor that ever has been in the land." [1]

Elizabeth, not wishing the execution of her favorite to boomerang, directed Bacon to write an exposition of the case. After revision by the queen, the account of Bacon was sent to the press on April 14, 1601, and appeared the same year from the press of Robert Barker, printer to the queen, with the title *A Declaration of the Practices and Treasons Attempted and Committed by Robert Late Earl of Essex*. In 1604, with James on the throne, Bacon again attempted to lay the ghost of Essex through the publication of *Sir Francis Bacon His Apologie, in Certaine Imputations concerning the Late Earle of Essex*.

I   A Declaration of the Practices and Treasons

A preface to the declaration states that false and corrupt relations of the legal proceedings, as well as lack of knowledge generally of the practices and inducements preceding the treason have

Apologist

made it proper to publish an account of the evidence, testimony, and confessions. Testimony was given that, through the conspiracy of Essex and the Irish rebel Tyrone, Essex was to become the king of England and Tyrone the viceroy of Ireland; the latter was to provide eight thousand Irish soldiers.[2] It was further developed that, when Essex went to Ireland, his heart was fraught with treason[3] and that a plot had been made to apprehend or execute Sir Walter Raleigh.[4] To the declaration proper is appended "The Effect of the Evidence," in which it is stated that twenty-five peers —a large number—sat in judgment. The evidence was handled in two parts: the plot of surprising the queen, and the open rebellion in the city. In another section, entitled "Some Particularities," it is stated that Essex likened his offense to "a leprosy that had infected far and near," and that he vehemently detested "his offence, desiring God to forgive him his great, his bloody, his crying, and his infectious sin."[5] In another division, "The Effect of That Which Passed at the Arraignments," it is stated that five conspirators "intended and compassed the death and destruction of the Queen's Majesty."[6] The last section entitled "The Confessions and Other Evidence" contains, among other confessions, that of Essex, in which he asked "God to forgive him his *great,* his *bloody,* his *crying,* and his *infectious sin*: which word *infectious* he privately had explained to us, that it was a leprosy that had infected far and near."[7]

Additional evidence not published with the declaration indicates that it was commonly rumored that "Anthony Bacon . . . was an agent between the Earl and the King of Scots, and so he was accounted."[8]

II Sir Francis Bacon His Apologie

About a year after Essex engaged in treason, Charles Blount, Lord Montjoy, afterwards the Earl of Devonshire, met Tyrone who was supported by Spanish troops, on Christmas Eve of 1601. Early in January, Montjoy defeated Tyrone decisively and placed himself in military command of all Ireland. In the summer of 1602, Bacon wrote a long letter to the queen's secretary, his cousin Sir Robert Cecil, recommending a course for transforming Ireland to a condition of civility.[9] The relics of war, he says, must be extinguished: the letting of blood should be minimized; a treaty

[89]

of peace should be made with Spain; and grace and pardon should be granted to those willing to be submissive.

The occupation forces should be tolerant "for a time not definite" of Roman Catholicism—a policy of necessity and one "warrantable by religion." Good preachers, "zealous persuaders," should be sent to Ireland; good bishops should be placed in the sees; religious works should be translated into the Irish tongue. Justice must be summary because Ireland must be administered through military government. The Irish people must be kept content and treated as if they and the English were one people; and great care must be taken in the education of the children. Great care also must be taken to eradicate seeds of trouble stemming from ambition of chiefs of families: licentious idleness of soldiers; and barbarous customs, including the savage enchantment of the people by their poets or heralds. Regarding plantations and buildings, fortifications should be constructed only for the control of the country; governors of towns should be "men gracious and well beloved, and are like to be well followed"; and the people should be encouraged to colonize various areas through "ample liberties and charters."

Had Elizabeth lived, she might have implemented Bacon's suggestions. But she died in 1603, and Bacon was constrained to explain to King James his entire relationship with Essex. It is probable, therefore, that Bacon wrote his *Apologie* in 1603 and that it was published early in 1604 in a diminutive volume; it was reprinted the following year. The distinguished military service of Montjoy was recognized by his appointment to the Lord Lieutenancy of Ireland and his creation as Earl of Devonshire. Since Montjoy had been closely associated with Essex, it was appropriate—and politically expedient—that Bacon address his *Apologie* to "The Right Honorable His Very Good Lord, the Earle of Devonshire, Lord Lieutenant of Ireland."

Toward the end of the *Apologie,* Bacon states that Elizabeth had commanded him to write the *Declaration;* that, after it had been printed, she had complained that he had referred to Essex as "My Lord of Essex" on almost every page; and that she commanded that it be printed anew and the subject referred to as "Essex, or the late Earl of Essex."

At the beginning of the work Bacon states that he is sensitive to

Apologist

the notion that he was false or thankless to Essex; that he recognizes the close friendship between Essex and Montjoy, as well as the schooling of the latter in duty and morality; and that whatever he, Bacon, did "was done in my duty and service to the Queen and the State; in which I would not shew myself false-hearted nor faint-hearted for any man's sake living. For every honest man, that hath his heart well planted, will forsake his King rather than forsake God, and forsake his friend rather than forsake his King; and yet will forsake any earthly commodity, yea and his own life in some cases, rather than forsake his friend," [10] Bacon continues: he was "not opposite to my Lord of Essex" but "did occupy the utmost of my wits, and adventure my fortune with the Queen to have reintegrated his." "I loved my country," Bacon says, "more than was answerable to my fortune, and I held at that time my Lord to be the fittest instrument to do good to the State; and therefore I applied myself to him in a manner which I think happeneth rarely amongst men." [11]

Continuing with the *Apologie*—personal, even intimate, in nature and contrasting sharply with the official tone of the *Declaration*—Bacon says that, when he had most power over Essex, the fortunes of Essex were greatest; that it was the belief of Essex that Elizabeth could be brought to action only by necessity and authority, but that he tried to persuade Essex that the only course to be followed with Elizabeth was that of obsequiousness; and that he had endeavored to dissuade Essex from seeking fame through military accomplishment.

With affection for both Essex and Elizabeth, Bacon tells of the sonnet that he had written, "though I profess not to be a poet," in the hope of reconciling the two. He also says that after Elizabeth had nominated Montjoy to the lord lieutenancy of Ireland, she spoke to Bacon about the appointment. "Madam," Bacon replied, "if you mean not to employ my Lord of Essex thither again, your Majesty cannot make a better choice." Her Majesty with passion interrupted, "Essex! whensoever I send Essex back again into Ireland, I will marry you, claim it of me." Bacon unmarried until 1606, relished the promise as well as his reply: "Well Madam, I will release that contract, if his going be for the good of your State." [12]

CHAPTER 11

A Book of Conduct for the Royalty

THE combination of man of action and man of contemplation in Bacon is at its best in his letters, advertisements, and recommendations to Queen Elizabeth and King James. The remarkable thing is not that Bacon dared admonish and advise such a benevolent tyrant as Elizabeth but that she heeded him, even to the point of agreeing or disagreeing with him. His offers of advice were first made when he was a very young man. But he was never a "temerarious youth" because he was never a youth nor unreasonably reckless. He had, besides, the reputation of his family to defend; but he dared more than did his father or his uncle, perhaps because he had less to lose. Primarily, he dared because he believed sincerely that a thinking young man should have sound advice to offer, and that thinking older heads, even those that sometimes wore crowns, should accept admonition. Not because Elizabeth felt close to the Bacon family but because she felt that the ideas of Bacon might be inherently good, the queen welcomed admonition concerning the affairs of church and state.

King James—closer to Bacon in age, education, and cool reasoning—usually took Bacon's advice with equanimity but with no zeal for acting on it; sometimes he hurled it back into the teeth of the adviser. The advice given by Bacon to James was usually on matters in which James had both personal and official interest: the union of England and Scotland, the pacification of the Church of England and its relationship to Puritanism, and the manifold problems in the administration of Irish affairs.

I *A Young Man Admonishes the Queen*

"Laying aside all self-guilty conceits of ignorance . . . , I will with the same sincerity display my humble conceits, wherewith my life shall be among the foremost to defend the blessing which

A Book of Conduct for the Royalty

God in you hath bestowed upon us." So Bacon, a fledgling diplomat then but twenty-three or twenty-four, began his "Letter of Advice to Queen Elizabeth."[1] The Papists, Bacon warns the queen, are your "strong factious subjects." He advises that they be required to take an oath of loyalty to the nation, but he would not make them desperate or even discontent. Turning from domestic enemies, he advises that France be converted from enmity to friendship; as for Scotland, there need be no fear of foreign aid while that country remained Protestant; but Spain is cause for alarm because of its religion and its close tie with Rome and because the king is loved by the malcontents of England.

Nothing is known of the use made of another paper written in 1589 and called "An Advertisement touching the Controversies of the Church of England."[2] Accepting the existence of controversies, Bacon says that the ancient and true bonds of unity are one faith and one baptism, not one ceremony and one policy. The causes of controversy usually are, first, the making of occasion for controversy; second, the extension and multiplication of it; third, the passionate and unbrotherly activity of each side toward the other; fourth, the drawing of the partisans of each side into a stricter union; and, fifth, the unnecessary propounding, publicizing, and debating of controversy.

After the defeat of the Spanish Armada, an attempt was made in England to control the Roman Catholics through legislation. A work attributed to Father Parsons—called *Responsio ad edictum Reginae Angliae* and accusing Elizabeth of creating all the disturbances in England and all Christendom—was answered by Francis Bacon in *Certain Observations Made upon A Libel Published This Present Year, 1592* [1593, present calendar].[3] The work opens with the thesis that in warfare nothing should be done to violate the law of nations or the law of honor, and that the good name of each participant should be preserved. England, it has been said, has never before had such miseries; but such a statement is false, for Almighty God has led Queen Elizabeth to the throne and to a flourishing hitherto unknown. The three scourges of God—war, famine, and pestilence—are offset by the three benedictions: peace, plenty, and health, which abound in England. Religion is pure; money is fine; and the navy so splendid through trade and discovery that the island has become the

Lady of the Sea. Concerning violence against Catholics, Elizabeth has been very lenient in dealing with them, having adopted the policy that consciences are not to be forced but to be won by truth.

The use to be made of Bacon's *A True Report of the Detestable Treason, Intended by Dr. Roderigo Lopez,* or the purpose for which it was written is unknown.[4] Early in 1594 Essex had uncovered a plot of the Spaniards who were using as their tool Dr. Roderigo Lopez, personal physician to the queen, to poison Elizabeth. A search of the house of the physician brought to light no incriminating evidence, whereupon Elizabeth condemned Essex, who thereafter did gather abundant evidence against Lopez. Bacon's account of the case, made from notes taken at the trial, was not published until 1657 in the *Resuscitatio.* Bacon establishes a good case against Lopez from the very beginning when he suborned various Englishmen and Irishmen through corrupting them with promises and money.

On the basis of internal evidence, an account of another attempt upon the life of the queen, and the life of Essex, is ascribed to Bacon: *A Letter Written Out of England to An English Gentleman Remaining in Padua, Containing a true report of a strange Conspiracy contrived between Edward Squire, lately executed for the same treason, as actor, and Richard Wallpoole, a Jesuit, as deviser and suborner, against the person of the Queen's Majesty. Imprinted by the deputies of C. Barker, 1599.*[5] This work was probably actually published in late December, 1598. Squire, a scrivener of Greenwich, had been employed in the queen's stable before going to the Indies on the last voyage of Sir Francis Drake. Captured by the enemy, he was taken as a prisoner of war to Spain but was soon set at liberty. Walpole determined to make Squire his tool, for he would return to England as a prisoner and not as a fugitive to poison Elizabeth and Essex. He gave to Squire two bladders of poison, one of which was placed upon the pommel of the queen's saddle and the other in the seat of a chair used only by the Earl of Essex aboard a ship in which Essex sailed. Neither intended victim was poisoned. The conspirators with Walpole believed that Squire had played them false and informed against him.

A Book of Conduct for the Royalty

II An English Gentleman Advises a Scottish King

Bacon presented to King James "at his first coming in" a writing entitled *Certain Considerations Touching the Better Pacification and Edification of the Church of England*.[6] Published in 1604, it was "Dedicated to his Most Excellent Majesty." Bacon, aware of dissensions within the church, begins his paper: "The unity of your Church, excellent Sovereign, is a thing no less precious than the union of your kingdoms." To the conventional Anglican, Bacon's faith was Puritanical, having been tinctured by the views of both mother and father; to the Puritan, he was liberal. In the belief that a Scotsman would not scorn the Puritan as did the Anglican, Bacon wrote what he believed to be true and wrote, therefore, his best work on ecclesiastical polity. Why, he asked, should "the civil state . . . be purged and restored by good and wholesome laws made every third or fourth year" while "the ecclesiastical state should still continue upon the dregs of time" for "five and forty years and more?" God, he said, "left the like liberty to the Church-government, as he hath done to the civil government." Apropos of a learned ministry, Bacon would not permit any with the "boldness to speak an hour together in a Church upon a text" to be "admitted for a preacher, though he mean never so well." Excommunication is "the greatest judgment upon the earth" and is not "to be used unreverently, and to be made an ordinary process to lackey up and down for fees" without "derogation to God's honour." Bacon ends the work with the prayer to God, "devout and fervent," that, "as he hath made your Majesty the cornerstone in joining your two kingdoms, so you may be also as a cornerstone to unite and knit together these differences in the Church of God."

The only reforms advocated are the elimination of ornate church music but the retention of the singing of psalms and spiritual songs; discontinuance as unnecessary of confirmation; disuse of the ring in a marriage ceremony; abandonment of the cap and surplice; and the forbidding of private baptism by laymen. All these things had been asked of James in a petition presented to him on his 1603 progress to London. But James later announced to the Puritans that he would have only one religion in substance and ceremony. The printed version of Bacon's considerations on pacification was called in.

A Brief Discourse Touching the Happy Union of the Kingdoms of England and Scotland, "Dedicated in private to His Majesty," was published by Bacon in 1603.[7] More than two-thirds of the work is devoted to a scholarly discussion of things in general and sometimes to union, like that of the Roman and the Sabine. Only at the end of the work does he speak of four types of union of kingdoms: name, language, laws, employments. Name is but a "superficial and outward matter"; language is unimportant because there is but one language, though of several dialects, in England and Scotland; the laws, both ecclesiastical and civil, have a fundamental uniformity; and regarding employments, just as the greater draws the lesser as when the greater light drowns the lesser, and just as time settles all things as in liquors which are at first troubled but grow clear in time, they will blend and lose agitation.

Bacon in 1604 bustled about the House of Commons on behalf of the union of England and Scotland. He analyzed the problems and raised a number of questions concerning the union in *Certain Articles or Considerations Touching the Union of the Kingdoms of England and Scotland. Collected and dispersed for his Majesty's better Service.*[8] He wondered whether laws relative to Scotland while the kingdoms were severed should be repealed; what laws, commissions, garrisons, and the like should be discontinued on the borders of both realms; and, the king's having considered these two questions, whether he should not stop and proceed no further toward a union. The nations are already united, Bacon says, in soveignty, subjection, religion, continent, language, and leagues and confederacies. But the nations are yet separate in external points: in ceremonial crowns; in names and appellations; in prints of seals, and in the marking of coins. In internal points they are still separate in the maintenance of separate parliaments, counsels of state, officers of the crown, nobilities, laws, justice, finances, admiralties, liberties, and taxes.

"The stile and title of King of Great Britany, France, and Ireland" should be used by King James, Bacon says in *A Draught of a Proclamation Touching His Majesty's Stile,* "Prepared, Not Used."[9] On October 20, 1604, a proclamation, seemingly an almost complete rewriting of that of Bacon, was made public.

A Book of Conduct for the Royalty

But Bacon was not neglectful of Ireland, particularly of the wilder northern part of the nation. To the king he addressed *Certain Considerations Touching the Plantation in Ireland*.[10] Although on the manuscript it is stated that the work was presented to the king in 1606, such a date is not possible; January, 1609, has been accepted as the probable date. The first publication was in 1657 in the *Resuscitatio*. Bacon opens with the observation that God has given King James two tasks: the union of England and Ireland, and the establishment of plantations in Ireland. Such plantations will bring honor to the king; homes for excess population of England and Scotland; strength against foreign enemies; and profit and strength to the crown, with first fruits to the king and with "a growing and springing vein of riches and power" to his posterity.[11]

CHAPTER 12

Biographer

WITH Tacitus, Bacon was convinced that the fundamental purpose of biography is to perpetuate virtuous behavior. To him, therefore, biography was a branch of literature and not of history. "I do find strange that these times have so little esteemed the virtues of the times," he says in the *Advancement of Learning*, "as that the writing of lives be no more frequent . . . yet are there many worthy persons that deserve better than dispersed report or barren eulogies." Believing as he did that biography must be a "true, native, and lively representation," Bacon leaned away from true biography—despite his feeling for history—and toward applied biography.

Bacon's biographic portraits are living men and women framed in the background of their times. Only in this sense is he the father of English biography. In English literature the stream of biography flows swiftly and has many tributaries. There are numerous early biographies, of which Bede's *Life of St. Cuthbert* and Asser's *Life of Alfred the Great* are important. More modern are the life of Sir Thomas More by both William Roper and Nicholas Harpsfield, which, together with George Cavendish's *Life of Wolsey*, probably gave inspiration to Bacon. But in subject and in style, the lives of Edward II and Richard III are more nearly prototypes of Bacon's biographies. Bacon's portraits, although intended to be complimentary, are more than hagiography and more than memoirs: they are based on intelligent, industrious research.

I Queen Elizabeth

Bacon's association with Queen Elizabeth was not so placid as he might have wished, but he sincerely lamented her death. Like the courtier-gentleman that he was, he welcomed King James to England; but he knew, judicious as he was, that friendship to a

Biographer

successor does not require dispraise of a predecessor. Bacon, looking back, praised Elizabeth in the first book of his *Advancement of Learning;* he said that she was an assiduous student, with profound knowledge in science, in modern and ancient language, and in divine and human law. The harvest of her wise government was forty-five years of unparalleled happiness.

Earlier, however, soon after her death, when he might have used his pen to his own advantage in praising the new king, he wrote *In Felicem Memoriam Elizabethae Angliae Reginae,* popularly called *The Felicity of Queen Elizabeth.* Bacon wrote this work in Latin for reasons that are not certain, but it is reasonable to assume that there were a number of them: elsewhere, he has said that modern languages might make bankrupts of all books; Latin was the universal language and that of the scholarly author; Latin more than English might honor the memory and the scholarly nature of the queen; and the work written in Latin might be included as a part of a monumental history being published in France at the time. Bacon says that Elizabeth attained sovereignty from private station. Henry VIII, he says, in attempting to excuse the execution of Anne Boleyn, was "by nature extremely prone both to loves and suspicions, and violent in both even to the shedding of blood." Bacon honors the appearance and way of life of Elizabeth; her maintenance of peace among a bellicose people, her moderation in religious struggle and her personal devoutness; and her courage in facing death. He concludes with the statement that time "has produced nothing in this sex like her, for the administration of civil affairs." The suppressions and emphases intended to honor the memory of Elizabeth make the work less than a judicial appraisal. A number of Roman Catholics were unhappy about Bacon's belief that Elizabeth was moderate in dealing with the Papist problem, and even his best friend, Tobie Matthew, took exception to this part of the biography.

Bacon thought so well of his biography of Elizabeth that, as his chaplain Dr. Rawley wrote in 1657, he planned in one draft of his will to have it published soon after his death. In a letter to the English ambassador to France, Sir George Carew, Bacon said that he would be pleased, in order that posterity might properly evaluate Elizabeth, to have Jacques Auguste de Thou, canon of Notre Dame and French historian, include *In Felicem Memoriam Eliz-*

abethae in *Historia sui Temporis*, then being issued. De Thou, with two brothers acting as librarians, brought together a tremendous library in Paris and there devoted most of his life to the writing of the *History of His Own Times*. But the Frenchman also had difficulties with the Papal See and others: the first eighteen books, published in 1604, were attacked by those whom the author called the envious and the factious; the second part, dealing with the first wars of religion, was put on the *Index Librorum Prohibitorum*, but it does not appear that inclusion in the list of books the reading of which was prohibited to Roman Catholics made the second part less popular than the other parts; the third part going to 1574, was published in 1607; and the fourth part, to 1584, in 1608. De Thou, as a complement to his history and as an explanation of that work, wrote his *Mémoires*. He, like Bacon, wished to produce a work of universal interest, one written without prejudice and as a result of purely scientific research. De Thou's failure to include Bacon's biography was not unfortunate for the reputation of Bacon. In England in 1651 T. Newcomb printed for George Latham a small volume entitled *The Felicity of Queen Elizabeth and her times, with other things, by the Right Honourable Francis Lord Bacon, Viscount St. Alban.*[1]

To William Camden's *Annals of Queen Elizabeth* Bacon contributed a number of manuscript corrections, none particularly important or interesting except for those in connection with the trials of Roderigo Lopez and of Essex.[2] Thomas Hearne included many of Bacon's corrections in his 1717 edition of Camden's work.

II Henry VIII, Edward, Mary, and Elizabeth

In Felicem Memoriam Elizabethae was written after the death of Elizabeth. Even earlier, during the reign of Elizabeth, Bacon began a work, never completed, entitled *The History of the Reign of K. Henry the Eighth, K. Edward, Q. Mary and Part of the Reign of Q. Elizabeth*. In the manuscript Bacon says that his intention is to give a picture "of a king that first, or next the first, became absolute in the sovereignty: of a king in minority: of a queen married to a foreigner: and lastly of a queen that hath governed without the help either of a marriage or any mighty man of her blood." Such comparison and contrast is the nucleus of Ba-

Biographer

con's biographic work. As with De Thou, Bacon finds his own time propitious because of the universal importance of England, the "new discoveries and navigations abroad," and the "new accidents memorable both of state and of court." In the second book of the *Advancement of Learning* Bacon speaks of the need of a history "from the Uniting of the Roses to the Uniting of the Kingdoms," or, in other words from Henry VII to James I; but such work had to be delayed until Bacon's fall from power. During the reign of Elizabeth, Bacon began an outline of the life of Henry VII in preparation for writing the life of Henry VIII, but he stopped, probably because of the burden of official duties. But the sketch of Henry VII did appear in print: it was used as a preface to Speed's history of the reign of Henry VII published in 1609.

Bacon attempted to please Prince Charles, the son of King James, who asked that he write a life of Henry VIII. Only a few pages of *The History of the Reign of King Henry the Eighth* are extant. They were published in 1629 by Bacon's chaplain, Dr. William Rawley, in *Certain Miscellany Works of the Right Hon. Francis Lord Verulam, Viscount St. Alban*. Ill health, Bacon says in a letter of October 22, 1623, has delayed his work on the biography. He had difficulty, moreover, in obtaining proper materials. His friend and fellow bibliophile, Sir Robert Bruce Cotton, he sadly says is "somewhat dainty of his materials in this." [3] As in his portrait of Elizabeth, so here Bacon says that her father Henry lacked relatives upon whom to depend for advice; he describes Henry's physical appearance, his eclipsing of his subjects, and his astuteness in international affairs. The mere framework of a life of Henry VIII is concluded with a tribute to the king, the wonder of the age.

III Henry VII

Bacon had returned to the life of Henry VII after his fall in 1621. This life was to be the first chapter of a proposed "History of England from the Union of the Roses to the Union of the Crowns," the need for which he had spoken in the *Advancement of Learning*. He must do honor to his country, he said, since he was no longer able to give service to it. He sent a copy of his life of Henry VII, whom James considered the ideal king, to the daughter of James, the queen of Bohemia, on April 20, 1622, with the pledge that he would not "become an abbey-lubber . . . but" would certainly "yield some fruit of my private life." [4]

The intention of Bacon was to show similarity between Henry VII and James. He was, he wrote to James on October 8, 1621, "in a sort your forerunner, . . . whose spirit, as well as his blood is doubled upon your majesty." [5] "I have not flattered him," Bacon says in a dedication to Prince Charles, "but took him to life as well as I could, sitting so far off, and having no better light. It is true, your Highness hath a living pattern, incomparable of the King your father. But it is not amiss for you also to see one of these ancient pieces." Even though Bacon was working in light and shade—light to illumine the virtues of his two characters, and shade to soften defects—he was so essentially truthful that he painted the best portrait of Henry in existence.

Even though Bacon had, in a letter of April, 1605, to Lord Chancellor Ellesmere conceived of a history of Great Britain—while contemplating the unworthiness of all English history and the partiality of Scottish history,—which would honor King James, now that the nations were united. Bacon had turned from such project because his fortune and his profession disqualified him; he, nevertheless, with freedom turned to the treasure houses of information about Henry VII: to the bountiful library of Sir Robert Bruce Cotton and to the histories of Polydore Vergil, Bernard André, Fabyan, Hall, Holinshed, Stowe, and Speed, and thus became one of the earliest of the modern English research scholars. The manuscript of *The History of the Reign of King Henry the Seventh* was completed in several months; it was then subjected to the correction of James. Covering the years 1485 to 1509, the book appeared in March, 1622, publication having been delayed at the request of the bishop of London. It was sold for six shillings.

The precision of research, the good judgment, and the grace of phrase gave this biography an academic and literary luster which yet remains. But, as in most other books, there are defects: Bacon castigates too gently the weaknesses of Henry, his marriage for expediency, his indifferent manner of dispensing justice except where he was a party, and his greed for gold. Henry is a politician, not a statesman. Bacon created speeches for Henry, some of which were extracted from Bacon's own speeches in Parliament;

Biographer

he praises the laws of Henry against enclosures, a subject upon which Bacon delivered several speeches. Sometimes the perspective is not so good as one might wish: too much space is given to unimportant details like the impersonations of Perkin Warbeck (a source of the works of Ford and Mary Shelley) and Lambert Simnel.

In *King Henry the Seventh* Bacon used framework and phraseology similar to that used in other biographies:

> *In Felicem Memoriam Elizabethae:* . . . she was raised to sovereignty from a private fortune.
> *The History of the Reign of King Henry the Eighth, King Edward, Queen Mary, and Part of the Reign of Queen Elizabeth:* This king [Henry VII] attained unto the crown, not only from a private fortune, which mought endow him with moderation, but also from the fortune of an exiled man, which had quickened in him all seeds of observation and industry.
> *Henry VII:* He attained to the crown, not only from a private fortune, which might endow him with moderation; but also from the fortune of an exiled man, which had quickened in him all seeds of observation and industry.

But each sovereign is individualized through careful selection of detail. Henry VII becomes a vital human being, and not a mere personage of history, through the inclusion of homely qualities. Much like the marmoset in Sir Thomas More's *Utopia*, Bacon includes a monkey which tore up Henry's notebook; Henry disliked entertainment; he expended vast sums on buildings; his relationship to the queen "was nothing uxorious"; he loved peace and religion. Henry VII, lying in Westminster in one of the stateliest monuments in Europe, Bacon says, "dwelleth more richly dead . . . than he did alive," and adds, "I could wish he did the like in this monument of his fame." He has come to do so. Rawley says that this biography achieved more fame abroad than at home And Bacon knew the merit of the work. The king had given the manuscript to Lord Brooke, Fulke Greville; and, commending it, James had enjoined Greville to read it. He, in turn, directed that "care should be taken by all means for good ink and paper to print it in; for that the book deserved it." [6]

IV *Prince Henry*

The king's eldest son, Henry, Prince of Wales, died on November 6, 1612, at the age of nineteen. Soon thereafter Bacon wrote a eulogy of Henry entitled *In Henricum Principem Walliae Elogium Francisci Baconi,* first published by Thomas Birch in 1763 in an edition of the works of Bacon. Birch suggested that Bacon's biography may, like that of Elizabeth also written in Latin, have been intended for inclusion in the history of De Thou. Conventionally, Bacon praises the personal appearance and the religious nature of Henry; but he brings him to life when he says that "in speech" he was "somewhat slow, and as it were embarrassed," even though his questions and opinions "were ever to the point and argued no ordinary capacity."

V *King James*

In an undated letter seemingly written early in 1610, Bacon asks King James to give him hope of public office; if denied, he says, he must honor James "by writing some faithful narrative of your happy though not untraduced times, or by recompiling your laws." In another undated letter, like the first probably written in 1610 and included in Rawley's *Resuscitatio,* in which *The Beginning of the History of Great Britain* was first published, Bacon tells the king that he is sending him a beginning of the history of his majesty's times. Bacon apologizes for not having been excessive because history forbids that an author "clutter together praises upon the first mention of a name, but rather disperseth and weaveth them" through the whole narrative.[7] Bacon wrote with great care of his living subject and used chiaroscuro, light and shade, effectively. He dared recall that difficult times were anticipated upon the death of Elizabeth; at that time the Essex faction rejoiced but the followers of Elizabeth shook with fear.

The biography lacks a physical portrait of James and a mental one based on attitudes and reactions to situations. Bacon closes with praise of *Basilikon Doron,* a work by James for the guidance of Prince Henry. Bacon says that this work, on the nature of kingship, is "a good perfume or incense before the King's coming in." He had written a declaration to prepare for the coronation of James, but he swallowed his embarrassment and said that the

Biographer

book was more worthy than a formal edict or declaration could have been. Sir Henry Wotton, after the death of Bacon, was commissioned to complete the work; but, after a beginning, he too died.

To his friend Tobie Matthew, Bacon on June 26, 1623 expressed the hope that this biography, together with other works, might be "well translated into Latin by the help of some good pens which forsake me not. For these modern languages will at one time or other play the bank-rowtes with books." [8]

VI The Character of Julius Caesar; The Character of Augustus Caesar

In *The History of the Reign of K. Henry the Eighth, K. Edward, and Q. Mary, and Part of the Reign of Q. Elizabeth,* Bacon says that he did "not attempt to go higher to more ancient times" because a previously written chronicle "as a simple narration of the actions themselves," which needed to be supplemented only by "the counsels and the speeches and the notable particularities," did "more and more fail." Yet the translation by Sir Thomas North of Plutarch's *Lives* in 1579 must have impressed Bacon to the extent that he decided to experiment with brief biographies of the ancients; and in his own writing he had established precedent in writing *De Sapientia Veterum.* His two brief biographies, written in semi-fictional and antithetic style, are to history what the *Essays* and *Of the Wisdom of the Ancients* are to philosophy. *Imago Civilis Julii Caesaris* appears to be complete, but it is probable that *Imago Civilis Augusti Caesaris,* even though it has unity, was not completed. Dr. Rawley, who included these biographies in his *Opuscula Posthuma* in 1658, says that they had been praised by men of great reputation. Bacon is content to narrate simply the personal character of the two ancients, but his studies are valuable in the stream of miniature biography.

CHAPTER 13

Advancement of Learning Divine and Humane

THE first king of England named James had come to the throne, but Bacon wrote to Cecil on July 3, 1603: "I desire to meddle as little as I can in the King's causes . . . My ambition now I shall only put upon my pen, whereby I shall be able to maintain memory and merit of the times succeeding."[1] Again the politician wrestled with the philosopher, the man of action with the man of contemplation.

I Experientia Literata *and* Interpretatio Naturae

Bacon's fecund mind and manual dexterity had already produced, during the spring and early summer of 1603, the proem of two prose handmaidens: *Experientia Literata* and *Interpretatio Naturae*. There are, Bacon says, three ways of advancing in learning: without plan, groping in the dark; proceeding from experiment to experiment; and following the light itself. Or, as he otherwise puts it, experiment should lead to experiment; axiom should lead to experiment; experiment should lead to the penetration of the mysteries of nature. Later, in the second book of the *Advancement of Learning,* he says that we are precluded from achieving the truth not because of the deception of the senses but because of the weakness of the faculties of the intellect and the manner of collecting and arriving at conclusions on the reports of the senses. He rejects the opinion of the Skeptics that it is not possible to arrive at certainty of knowledge, but he believes that the syllogism is not effective in solving the secrets of nature because the laws of nature are not reducible to the middle terms of the syllogism.

In the proem to *Of the Interpretation of Nature,* Bacon concedes that "without guide or light" he is entering "upon an argument of all others the most obscure," and that he is "a man not old"

Advancement of Learning Divine and Humane

but of "weak health" with his "hands full of civil business." Even so, he will dedicate his powers to this work because birth and education had designed him for state service. Zeal, he says, has been mistaken by some for his ambition; and, anticipating the charge of intellects less great that he was seeking to be "wise overmuch," he says that in contemplation the only criterion is truth, and that he was "fitted for nothing so well as for the study of Truth." In the proem he bares his thoughts and, without affected modesty, begins: "Believing that I was born for the service of mankind, and regarding the care of the commonwealth as a kind of common property which like the air and the water belongs to everybody, I set myself to consider in what way mankind might be best served, and what service I was myself best fitted by nature to perform."

II *Leave Aristotle and Artificiality*

To the Renaissance thinker, Aristotle and artificiality were synonymous. Nearly two thousand years before the English Renaissance Aristotle had divided learning into biology, ethics, physics, politics, and psychology; and, on the basis of inquiry, he had made observations on each. He had knowledge of inductive reasoning, but he relied too heavily upon the deductive syllogism. In *Redargutio Philosophiarum* or *The Refutation of Philosophies,* Bacon wrote: "Be not misled by the statement that Aristotle and others in old times practiced Induction and Experience. That so-called Induction was but an imposture." It was the theory of Aristotle that all heavenly bodies are constant and regular. At about the time that Bacon entered Cambridge, a new star had appeared in Cassiopeia, a region considered unchangeable by Aristotle; in 1574 the new star was extinguished, as was Bacon's faith in the theories of Aristotle. Twenty years later in *The Praise of Knowledge* (1592), Bacon says, "Who would not smile at Aristotle, when he admireth the eternity and invariableness of the heavens . . ."

But Aristotle must be placed in his era and evaluated according to the standards of his age. His induction is quite different from that of Bacon. He was, as Bacon points out, magnified by the Schoolmen, or by the medieval theologians, who enjoyed disputation. "The Schoolmen, having made Divinity into an art," Bacon says, "have almost incorporated the contentious philosophy of Aristotle into the body of Christian religion." [2] But not only the Schoolmen and other Aristotelians distorted the theories of Aristotle, which came in the thirteenth century to the University of Paris and Oxford and Cambridge—not direct but from Cordova, the seat of Arabic learning, in which Aristotle had been taught since 800, and from Constantinople, where his teaching had been popular from 1100. Because of this popularity and because Constantinople was the capital of the Ottoman empire, Bacon called Aristotle an Ottoman.

Even in the fourteenth century Chaucer smiles at his clerk of Oxford when he reads not only the works of Aristotle but also the works about those works, those "twenty bokes" of "Aristotle and his philosophye." It is no wonder that John Lyly, slight philosopher but strong dramatist, said that at Oxford he had nursed "at a drie breast three years." [3] It was not Aristotle, the Ottoman sultan, but his misguided followers, his unenlightened janizaries, who attributed to him the misconception that a measure of earth may be converted into ten of water, and one of water into ten of air.

III Sources of the Advancement of Learning

Out of chaotic nebulae Bacon desired to form a scientific cosmos in *The Two Bookes of Francis Bacon of the Proficience and Advancement of Learning Divine and Humane*, which he began in 1603 during a period of relative leisure. The work, published in 1605, summons all scholars to prayer for the advancement of the human mind even though Bacon modestly hopes to be but "like a bell-ringer, which is first up to call others to church." [4]

From old seed sown in earlier works, many of the concepts in the *Advancement* have sprung. At a time that Bacon was probably acting as secretary to Essex, the latter sent out a number of letters which Bacon may have composed, or which Essex may have dictated, or which may contain ideas conventional in that day. In any event, some of them germinated in the *Essays* and in the *Advancement*. One of them signed "E." was written in January, 1595–96, to the fifth earl of Rutland, the son-in-law of Sir Philip Sidney. It contains statements almost identical to some in "Of Studies" as well as the sentence, "The gifts or excellencies of the mind are the same as those are of the body; Beauty, Health, and Strength." This statement reappears in slightly different form in the second book of the *Advancement:* "We divided the good of the body into *health, beauty, strength,* and *pleasure;* so the good of the mind . . . tendeth to this, to make the mind *sound,* and without perturbation; *beautiful,* and graced with decency; and *strong* and *agile* for all duties of life."

Another letter by Essex complies with a request by Sir Fulke Greville for advice as to the nature of information to be collected for him by two of three assistants at Cambridge University. The letter contains many phrases later included in the *Advancement* and says that collections may be from readings (1) by epitome or abridgement, or (2) under heads and commonplaces, the latter being of more value. Greville, the letter says, should occupy himself in collecting the "chiefest things and out of the chiefest books," and the other collectors should gather "arguments and examples to prove or illustrate any particular position or question." [5]

But in the *Advancement* other old seed planted in *The Promus of Formularies and Elegancies* sprang up again. This work, published by Mrs. Henry Pott in London in 1883, is mainly in folio 114 in the British Museum and is headed "Formularies, Promus. 27 Jan. 1595." On the back of the folio is written "fragments of Elegancyes." This collection, begun on December 5, 1594, or earlier, and continued for at least two years, is a source of the lucid, sententious style of Bacon and of the aphorisms—or apophthegms, to use his word—rich in denotation and connotation for which Bacon is famous. Bacon recommends such collections in the second book of the *Advancement,* in which he defines *formulae* as "but decent and apt passages or conveyances of speech, which may serve indifferently for differing subjects; as of preface, conclusion, digression, transition, excusation, &c."

But the *Advancement* not only garners old seed from earlier works; it transmits them for planting in later works. In the *De Augmentis Scientiarum* (v, 5), for instance, he again advocates collections like those in *The Promus:* "I hold diligence and labour in the entry of commonplaces to be a matter of great use and support in studying." Similarly the *Advancement* is one of the sources of the *Novum Organum,* which, in turn, is the nucleus of the *Instauratio Magna.* In this manner, Bacon, the creator of a number of highly diversified works, has forged each work to another or all the others.

IV Structure and Style of the Advancement of Learning

"Heaven and earth," Bacon declares in the first book of the *Advancement of Learning*, "conspire and contribute to the use and benefit of man." The scientist, he says, is more concerned with the part than with the whole—a statement which would be even more true today, when the scientist often knows nothing of the nature of the whole or even that it exists; the philosopher, he says attractively while using an image from Plato, is like that wise man who while gazing at the stars fell into the water, even while he might have seen the stars reflected in the water. Changing his figure from the bell-ringer to two others regarding his desire, Bacon says that he wished to be but a signpost to Nature, the inventor not the operator of the machine which would lead to Nature.

This being his purpose, he must be judged on the basis of what he attempted to do and his success therein. He said frankly that he was entering without light the most obscure of recesses of Nature. He, therefore, must not be charged with insufficiency of knowledge of physics, mathematics, and the other sciences or that he made few experiments and none materially contributing to knowledge. Even his last experiment, that of stuffing a fowl with ice, was unoriginal because the ancients had established definitively that cold arrested putrefaction.

Nor should Bacon be condemned because his contribution to philosophy is the widow's mite: "I have no desire," he said, to found a sect, "after the fashion of heresiarchs." It must be accepted without objection that he neither founded nor adhered to any single system of philosophy. As a philoscientist, one who worked with love in both science and philosophy, Bacon immortalized himself. With greater vision than had the scientist, with keener insight into human need than had the philosopher of his day, Bacon neither crawled on his belly with the scientist nor soared on waxen wings into the heavens with the philosopher; he suspended himself midway between air and earth, and saw and pointed out the way in which he believed the mysteries of Nature might be penetrated for the alleviation of human burdens. Dismissing altogether the advance made in knowledge during the past third of a millennium—and even during the past three years —and the modern demand for results, negative as well as positive, in research, with the same experiments being conducted by hundreds of people, and placing Bacon in the early part of the seventeenth century, it must be granted that he was eminently successful in that he repudiated the spurious niceties of scholastic philosophy and directed the capture and confinement of Nature for the benefit of man.

Like the bronze statue of a famous sculptor, Bacon has molded a work of noble symmetry and heroic proportion, one which can weather all storms. It is architectonics, Goethe says, that distinguishes between the amateur and the artist. If this statement is true, Bacon is one of the few great artists in English literature. Before making a division of any main heading, he announces his subdivisions. In this work he says, "For as in buildings, there is great pleasure and use in the well-casting of the staircases, entries, doors, windows, and the like; so in speech, the conveyances and passages are of special ornament and effect." Like the good pilot, he never leaves the channel of the mainstream without pausing to show the relationship between it and the various bays and creeks which he is to sail upon, and he comments with learning and charm on all the landmarks on each shore. He has enriched his great work and ennobled it with the wizardry of words. In the *Advancement,* he abandoned the powerful but stark and lifeless style of the first edition of the essays and attained stylistic maturity.

In the *Advancement* are obsolete words of Greek ancestry taken from medieval Latin, like *systasis;* and words which have survived in modern English in another form, like *reluctation;* and words used humorously, like *celsitude;* and obsolete words like *illaqueation* and *colliquation;* and neologisms like *non-promovent.* Linguistically, the *Advancement* is for the average reader at times a Pandora's box; for the philologist, it is a treasure chest, a heritage of the Renaissance in which modest Germanic words like *moe* hang their heads and stately Latinisms like *suppeditation* try to overshadow them because the various languages contributing to the English language had not yet been melted into a single metal. Bacon preferred the Latinism to the Old English word because the Latinism is usually preferred by the philosopher and by the scientist. And it may be said without fear of overstatement that Bacon helped to fix the language of philosophy and science. The use of ancient words gave to Bacon's style uniqueness, gravity, and eloquence. But Bacon advises in the *Advancement* against studying words and neglecting the matter, for "Falling in love with words is falling in love with pictures." But we might apply to Bacon's written language what Henry Gosnold, a young lawyer of Gray's Inn, wrote to Anthony Bacon about his brother's spoken language: it was gracious for its propriety rather than strange for its novelty.

Bacon uses the axiom in the *Advancement* almost as effectively as he uses it in the *Essays,* and sometimes he repeats or varies slightly a maxim used in one of the essays. He has said, for instance, in "Of Atheism" virtually what he says in the *Advancement*: "A little or superficial knowledge of philosophy may incline the mind of man to atheism, but a farther proceeding therein doth bring the mind back again to religion." The axiomatic quality of Bacon's style makes him one of the most quotable authors.

Sometimes Bacon engages in play upon words, and sometimes he uses balance, antithesis, and an enchainment of clauses as did the Euphuists of his day. But he is not excessively precious as they are and as is own essays are. The subject matter exalts the *Advancement*. Unlike Edmund Spenser, who studiedly created archaisms with which he wove wreaths of artificial flowers, Bacon is more like—and perhaps set the pattern for—Milton in his plea for freedom of the press, except that Bacon is more open of mind and more eloquent in his fervent plea for freedom of knowledge.

To the language of the ancients, to natural history, to the rhetoric and the resounding vowels of the Bible, he went for inspiration:

> For as water, whether it be the dew of heaven, or the springs of the earth, doth scatter and lose itself in the ground, except it be collected into some receptacle, . . . so this excellent liquor of knowledge, whether it descend from divine inspiration, or spring from human sense, would soon perish and vanish to oblivion, if it were not preserved in books, traditions, conferences, and places appointed, as universities, colleges, and schools, for the receipt and comforting of the same.

That Nature must be subservient to man, is the nucleus of the *Advancement*, for too long has man been subservient to Nature.

Advancement of Learning Divine and Humane

The spirit of the Renaissance is strong in the *Advancement,* a survey and correlation of the sciences and an evaluation of existing knowledge with a view to determining how it is to advance. Knowledge of both the past and present must be organized, trained, and disciplined. Divines, politicians, and scholars themselves, Bacon says in Book I, have discredited learning. The divines, believing that learning inclined the mind to atheism, thought that it had besmirched religion. A thorough knowledge of philosophy, Bacon replies, leads not to atheism but to religion. The politicians had averred that learning weakens the mind and leads from the active to the contemplative life. But, Bacon retorts, the ages most famous in the history of nations for military distinctions were most famous for learning. With Plato, Bacon says that, when philosophers are kings, or kings philosophers, times will be happy. The scholars, those entrusted with learning, have failed because of their need for leading private lives, and because of their low station and poverty.

In general, learning, he says, has become delicate, fantastic, and contentious. Men strive for words rather than for thoughts—all their thoughts having been enclosed in a few books, particularly those of Aristotle. The imagination has taken the place of reason in the sciences; natural magic, astrology, and alchemy have been pursued rather than the true sciences; and learning has become tainted with untruth. All men are both antiquity and futurity: they must not follow one to the exclusion of the other. Men, mistaking the end of learning, have not exercised their minds for the benefit of mankind but for curiosity or entertainment, or for mental adornment, or for argument, or for material gain. Man must not beckon divine philosophy from the heavens to walk with men upon the earth; but, because "both heaven and earth do conspire and contribute to the use and benefit of man," he must reject what is void and garner and bring to fruit that which is sound.

Book I closes in praise of knowledge, of which "there is no satiety, but satisfaction and appetite are perpetually interchangeable"; in praise of the human mind, which is "settled, landed, and fortified in the certainty of truth," a quotation from Lucretius used also in the *Essays;* and in fear that, like Ulysses, who preferred his wife to immortality, humanity might prefer custom to excellence.

Book II of the *Advancement* is vastly more important than Book I, an introduction. But Book II is so complex that it could be surveyed better in outline form; indeed, the outline was Bacon's Jacobean map of learning. It must be granted that his cross-references are tedious, that it is sometimes difficult to follow the nebulous threads from one division of knowledge to another, and that his categorizing is sometimes inaccurate or questionable, but it must also be conceded that Bacon has charted intellectual seas and shore lines with genius. The boundaries of known lands are definite and detailed, of unexplored lands hazy but suggestive. Candidly he says that work in some fields has been adequate but that in other fields it has been deficient. The classification of knowledge in Book II was so valuable that it was followed in the eighteenth-century encyclopedia projected by Diderot. Because of the limitations of space, only a few words will be said here of the nature of the second book.

In the dedication to the king of Book II, Bacon says that learning should be applied to action. The nourishment of all professions being derived from philosophy, it is lamentable that all the colleges of Europe are devoted to professional work and none to arts and sciences generally. The curricula of the universities should be evaluated again; the practice of studying basic materials in abridged forms should be abandoned; there should be greater recompense for public lectures; and experimentation should be more common. Authors have too much devoted their efforts to explored and desiccated fields. There should be greater collaboration in learning among the various universities. Most of these defects, Bacon says, can be cured by a king; the private person can but point out the way.

Learning is divided on the basis of the faculties of the human mind; history is correlated to memory, poetry to imagination, philosophy to reason. Bacon defines poetry as

a part of learning in measure of words for the most part restrained, but in all other points extremely licensed, and doth truly refer to the Imagination; which, being not tied to the laws of matter, may at pleasure join that which Nature hath severed, and sever that which Nature hath joined, and so make unlawful matches and divorces of things. . . . It is taken in two senses, in respect of words or matter. In the first sense it is but a character of style, and belongeth to arts of speech, and is not pertinent for the present. In the later, it is (as hath been said) one of the principal portions of learning, and is nothing else but Feigned History, which may be styled as well in prose as in verse.

Much in advance of the medical theory and practice in the England of his day, Bacon in his discussion of science urges the recording of new ills and their treatment, and he suggests greater research in comparative anatomy and vivisection—studies that were being carried on in Italy in his day.

Man should not give the impression of having too much goodness, he says in the discussion of human conduct, but should show some spirit and even some edge.

Mere lawyers who know what the law is but not what it should be and visionary philosophers, but not statesmen, have devised the legal system and have debased it.

In the discussion of philosophy, he urges the use of more logic and of the inductive method, as well as a collection of ancient philosophies. There are two kinds of good, he says in discussing ethics, private and public, the latter being of greater value.

Book II, in which Bacon candidly reveals himself as man, lawyer, statesman, scientist, and philosopher, has value as a survey of knowledge; but it is also of great worth as a study of the deficiencies of knowledge. For the learned man, it is the greatest work of the century.

To King James, Bacon said that the first book deals with the excellence of learning and the second with the progress and defects of learning; and he said to his friend Tobie Matthew that the first book is but as a page to the second.

Openhanded with presentation copies, Bacon sent the *Advancement*, soon after its publication on November 7, 1605, to his college and to his university; to Oxford University and to Sir Thomas Bodley, whose library at Oxford was "an ark to save learning from deluge"; to the Earl of Northampton with the request that he present it to James, "the learnedst king that hath reigned"; to the Earl of Salisbury, Lord Treasurer Buckhurst, and Lord Chancellor Egerton; and he asked the professor of divinity at Cambridge University, Dr. Playfer, to translate the work into Latin. The Latin translation made eight books of the English version of the *Advancement of Learning*.

Book II was greatly expanded in the 1623 edition of the *Advancement*, to which Bacon suffixed "The Coast of the New Intellectual World; or, a Recapitulation of the Deficiencies of Knowledge, Pointed out in the Preceding Work, to be Supplied by Posterity." Three years before his death he had come to realize that his plan was so vast that he alone could not complete the work that he had envisioned. In the suffix he recommends a universal literary history; a universal biography; a philosophical history of the heavens; a monumental study of comparative anatomy; an exhaustive account of the various languages in order that a perfect, and common, language might result; and the establishment of a system for the dispensation of universal justice. Man yet waits for the fulfilment of Bacon's dream, but he has never questioned its worth.

CHAPTER 14

Cogitata et Visa *and* De Sapientia Veterum

IN addition to the *Advancement of Learning*, during the first decade of the seventeenth century Bacon wrote two other works, both of which he had in mind at the time that he composed the *Advancement*. Desiring an introduction to some tables that he had compiled and called *Legitimate Investigation of Motion*, he wrote a work called *Cogitata et Visa De Interpretatione Naturae, sive De Scientia Operativa*, or in English *Thoughts and Judgments concerning the Interpretation of Nature, or concerning Operative Science*. Under Human Philosophy in the *Advancement*, Bacon says that medicine is deficient because too many cases are reported to be incurable; toward the beginning of the *Cogitata et Visa* he says that, in too many cases, doctors have declared patients to be incurable. In both works he damns magicians and alchemists, and in both he discredits Aristotle, who, he says in the *Cogitata*, has corrupted natural philosophy by dialectic reasoning. The *Cogitata* was, therefore, intended to be followed, in its present form, by a second part (which is now contained in the second book of the *Novum Organum*) which would be a specimen of true inductive investigation.[1] In the *Cogitata* Bacon also enumerates the forces and persons which have hindered the propagation of learning in a manner very similar to that in which he sets them forth in Book I of the *Advancement*.

In an appendix to Natural Philosophy, Bacon recommends a collection of ancient philosophies and under Civil Knowledge he encourages the cultivation of ancient learning. In this general pattern may be placed *De Sapientia Veterum*.

I Cogitata et Visa

Bacon did become entangled in civil business, and he did not carry out his desire expressed in 1603 "to meddle as little as I can in the King's causes." He was appointed solicitor general in June, 1607. He, nevertheless, found a little leisure and began *Cogitata et Visa,* or *Reflections and Speculations.* But there were interruptions: his mother-in-law, Lady Pakington, seemingly enjoyed a slight rift between Lady Bacon and her husband, even to the extent that she declared that she would take back her daughter if she were cast off by Bacon. "For it is much more likely we have occasion to receive you being cast off, if you remember what is passed," Bacon replied in anger, "And you shall at this time pardon me this one fault of writing to you. For I mean to do it no more till you use me and respect me as you ought." [2] In late December, 1607, Bacon had to complain to an officer of the Exchequer that a grant by the king of a hundred pounds to him in the late fall had not been paid. Bacon's best friend, Tobie Matthew, son of the archbishop of York, had been imprisoned because of conversion to Catholicism. And such difficulties had arisen in Ireland that Bacon had to obtain intelligence from officials there. His philosophic reflection was agitated by such personal and semiofficial interruptions. The *Cogitata,* not published until 1653, was sent in manuscript form in 1607 to Sir Thomas Bodley for comment, and to an old friend Dr. Launcelot Andrews, who had been consecrated bishop of Chichester in 1605, for helpful, though severe, criticism such as Andrews had given of the *Advancement.*[3]

"Francis Bacon thought thus," the *Cogitata et Visa* begins. What he thought is important to an understanding of his philosophy: the mechanical arts have not sought much light from philosophy. That which the physician has not attained, he declares to be unattainable. Aphorisms were garnered in storehouses of truth by the earliest seekers for truth, and those who followed them were invited to criticism and invention. But now in science the master-disciple relationship exists, not that of inventor and continuer. Today, Bacon says, men seek knowledge for delight, profit, or ornament—an idea much like that in "Of Studies"—but the true end of knowledge should be to enrich mankind with new works and powers. Philosophy, the great mother of science, has been transmuted into a maidservant because, after the Christian faith had come to maturity, the best minds turned to theology, just as the Romans turned to civil affairs. Excessive superstition and immoderate, blind zeal of religion have toppled natural philosophy; and

Cogitata et Visa *and* De Sapientia Veterum

man has come to fear that inquiry into the mysteries of Nature might reveal something destructive of religion.

The development of science in the schools and colleges has been deliberately impeded, and study has been limited to certain authors. Leaders of the people have kept to themselves knowledge of the sciences, and the knowledge of man has been mocked by the use of words vague in meaning or ill defined. Some have even come to believe that the mind is dulled by experimentation and that knowledge comes from within and not from the senses. New ideas have been kept out of natural philosophy because of the prejudices of men against the new philosophic concepts. Some of the men celebrated in that day—men like William Gilbert, physician-physicist, typical of the Renaissance, whose work on the magnet was published in 1600 and whose *New Physiology* Bacon had probably seen in manuscript form—said a few things of importance; but they did not see the truth; they trifled with Nature without making a close union with her. Incomplete and unreliable, he says, are the methods of demonstration then in use; demonstrations should not be restricted to the senses but should be corrected by the enlightened intellect. Men must consider whether they should overthrow their old methods and establish new ones.

Just as Bacon expected more from old men than from young, so the age should have produced more because of reliance on past discoveries. Progress in science has been made because of a number of things, including religious controversies because man has turned from them in repulsion back to his studies; and the improvement in literature, progress in printing, and peace have made great contribution to such progress.

The empire of man lies in knowledge alone. All men have three ambitions: to increase their power in their own country, to increase the power of their country among other nations, and to extend the power of man over the universe of matter. The third is, of course, the most admirable.

The philosophies of the Greeks, and especially of Aristotle, Bacon says, have been like the arguments of dramatic pieces belonging to fiction. Aristotle thought that the syllogism took the place of an oracle but failed to recognize that the syllogism consists of mere propositions, and propositions of mere words—words which are the tokens and signs of the ideas or thoughts of the mind. Therefore, if the ideas themselves, which are the life of the words, were vague, unknown, or not sufficiently defined, which is for the most part very much the case in Nature—everything sinks. Even the helpless hand may, with the aid of the compass, draw a perfect circle; likewise the mind must seek a compass, not in the deductive syllogism but in the new induction. The old induction, which is but water to the wine of the new induction, contains a middle proposition arrived at deductively through reasoning of the syllogism. Only the name of induction, Bacon says, is known; men have hidden its use and force. Recognizing the danger of jumping from particulars to general comprehensions, Bacon believes, nevertheless, that scholars should not go from particulars digested into tables to new particulars; they should proceed to general comprehensions. A form of induction should be introduced in which general conclusions may be reached from certain particulars, proving that there may not be found a contradictory instance. His method, Bacon admits, is one of performance rather than opinion. As he has before said, he recognizes the fact that he is not founding a particular school of thought; he is interested in utility and in the enlargement of knowledge.

Equally important as the discovery of knowledge are communication and transmittal. That there may be in the future no need for a leader, Bacon is, he declares, preparing a work on Nature in which he is bringing and scattering light from Nature herself. The best method of attracting attention to the new induction is to offer a mass of particulars, or tables of discovery, or aphorisms; but it would be abrupt to present such tables without introduction. He has prepared, therefore, the *Cogitata* as a preface.

II *Interludes:* Commentarius Novus *and* Transportata

Conforming to his practice of making notes on all that he had read or thought and of periodically discarding, condensing, or transferring such notes as had not been used, Bacon transferred from July 25 to July 31, 1608, from temporary notes to semipermanent form ideas which had come to his mind from time to time. He called the collection *Commentarius Solutus, Miscellaneous* [literally, loose] *Commentary;* and he said that it was "like a merchant's waste-book; where to enter all manner of remem-

Cogitata et Visa *and* De Sapientia Veterum

brance of matter, form, business, study, touching myself, service, others; either sparsim or in schedules, without any manner of restraint; only this to be divided into two books: The one *transportata ex commentario vetere,* containing all manner notes already taken in several paper books fit to be retained (except it be such as are reduced to some more perfect form); the other *Commentarius novus."*

Because these notes were made for his own contemplation and not to be seen by others, they mirror the man, private and public, much better than do his letters, his speeches, and his formal works. The *Commentary* is a storehouse of information, trivial and important, about Bacon's hopes—personal, political, philosophical, and literary. Like the intellectual of today, he has no fear of his own image: he uses other people to his own advantage —even the king; yet he is a monarchist, and prefers the will of the king to that of the people; but, even though he likes the Parliament, it must be subjected to the will of the people.

Like the *New Commentary,* the *Transportata,* or *Things Transferred from Old Commentaries* (now in the British Museum) contains reflections upon public and private matters, and is a frank, and at times unintelligible, statement of thoughts which passed through Bacon's mind. In places it reveals him as a petty, overzealous man; but it also reveals his love of Nature and of country.

We are led to believe from statements in the *Transportata* and elsewhere that Bacon conceived a plan for the *Instauratio Magna* at about the time he wrote *Cogitata et Visa.* In the *Transportata* he shows an interest in securing patronage for the *Instauratio* and in obtaining aid in his study by appealing to the reason and imagination of men and by presenting results of his new method of the study of Nature. As in the *New Atlantis,* and even in his will, Bacon wished to found a technical college and to subsidize scholarship in science. Moreover, the wilds of Scotland should be colonized; Ireland should be civilized; the church should be restored to earlier authority; laws should be collected; and the king and parliament should be turned from dispute to public problems.

Bacon is also interested in his health. He lists minor works completed, in progress, or projected. He estimates his assets at 24,155 pounds, with a yearly income of 4,975, and his liabilities at 4,481 pounds. He will surround his house at Gorhambury with a brick wall; he will build an artificial lake with an island a hundred feet wide, and upon the island he will put up a summerhouse—not a rustic structure but one with galleries, a supping room, and a music room. He will also build other islands, one with rock and one with flowers arranged in ascent, each island to have a statue to distinguish it from other islands.

Scraps of Latin mingled with English, sometimes arbitrarily abbreviated, indicate a desire to be appointed administrator of the estates of his half-sister, formerly Lady Neville, and of Lady Dorset, the widow of Thomas Sackville, or to be executor of the wills of their husbands.

He desires, he says, to finish his work on "ye Great. of Br.," which he had evidently begun. *Of the True Greatness of the Kingdom of Britain*, an early excursion into geopolitics, was not completed. Many of the ideas contained therein appear in his essay "Of the True Greatness of Kingdoms and Estates," and in Latin in *De Augmentis Scientiarum*. His work, though never completed, was dedicated to King James and was first published in 1634.

III   Concerning the Wisdom of the Ancients

In the *Cogitata et Visa* Bacon says that he could have palmed off new discoveries as rediscoveries of the earlier Greeks but he objected to imposture.

"You are right in supposing that my great desire is to draw the sciences out of their hiding-places into the light," Bacon wrote to the great scholar Isaac Casaubon, then in Paris. "So I seem to have my conversation among the ancients more than among these with whom I live." [4] He seemed to believe that earlier Greek philosophers like Pythagoras and Democritus had penetrated some of the secrets of Nature, and that the myths of religion and the stories of the Greek poets contain mysteries, often political. Parabolic poetry is used, Bacon says in the *Advancement of Learning*, when "the secrets and mysteries of religion, policy, or philosophy are involved in fables or parables"; and "I do rather think that the fable was first and the exposition devised, than that the moral was first and thereupon the fable framed." The ideas of the preceding sentences are the nuclei of *De Sapientia Veterum*, or *Concerning the*

Cogitata et Visa *and* De Sapientia Veterum

Wisdom of the Ancients. He condensed and retold stories from Classical mythology, and he gave to the stories such interpretation as would make his own concepts of politics, science, philosophy, and religion acceptable—indeed welcome—to his readers. Toward the close of the fable of Prometheus, Bacon says, "Such are the views which I conceive to be shadowed out in this so common and hacknied fable."

A few examples of the use made by Bacon of the ancient fables will be sufficient: the rebellion by the Giants against Jupiter represents sedition annihilated by sovereignty; the story of Diomedes is the story of men who overthrow religious worship; Styx symbolizes treaties and compacts of princes; and Narcissus denotes self-love and represents those persons who live sheltered lives, surrounding themselves with a few friends who echo their voices. In like manner, Bacon interprets all the thirty-one fables to deal with kingship, religion, war, human conduct, and philosophy.

The interpretations of Bacon of ancient myths are not accepted as true today because he used them for a special purpose: he worked ideas into the parables which had become fixed in his own mind.

Concerning the Wisdom of the Ancients is related to the *Essays* in that they set forth ideas that Bacon had considered, but the method is different from that used in the *Essays* because both positive and negative arguments are not presented. "The Greek tragic writers," Shelley in a similar manner declares in his preface to *Prometheus Unbound,* "in selecting as their subject any portion of their . . . mythology . . . by no means conceived themselves bound to adhere to the common interpretation or to imitate in story as in title their rivals and predecessors." Bacon, however, thought that the ancient myths had been received and believed at the time that they were used by ancient authors, even by Homer and Hesiod, and that some of them had been adorned and given a new allegory; and he says in his preface that his efforts would be rewarded by "throwing light either upon antiquity or upon nature itself."

De Sapientia Veterum was published in Latin in 1609 by Robert Baker. On February 17, 1609–10, Bacon sent a copy to Tobie Matthew with the statement that "They tell me my latin is turned into silver, and become current." The book contains a dual dedication; the first is to his cousin, the Earl of Salisbury, chancellor of Cambridge University, in which he says that he holds philosophy "of all things, next to religion, the most important and most worthy of human nature." The second dedication is to "his nursing-mother the famous University of Cambridge," in which he says that, without philosophy, he cares not to live, and that he believes it but appropriate that what came from Cambridge should return thereto. But remembering the uninspired learning that he received at Cambridge, he adds sadly: "There are few footprints pointing back towards you, among the infinite number that have gone forth from you."

CHAPTER 15

Novum Organum

IN 1620 Bacon published his work originally called *Key of the Interpretation of Nature,* or by its new name, the *Novum Organum,* a work which his chaplain, Dr. Rawley, says he saw revised twelve times during twelve successive years. Never completed, it was at first intended to be the second part of the *Instauratio Magna;* but moral and political treatises, more nearly ready for publication, were substituted for it. In an introduction Bacon explains that the work was published in unfinished condition because he wished, in the event of his death, to leave an outline of his great project. On the title-page appears *Magna Instauratio,* the title of the entire work of which the *Novum Organum* was to be but a part. After a dedication to the king and a general preface, a *distributio operis,* or arrangement of the work, appears; the arrangement is, however, not that of the *Novum Organum* but of the entire *Instauratio Magna.*

The title, ironically, is taken from Aristotle—ironic because Bacon's method is inductive; Aristotle's, deductive. Whether or not conscious of the philosophic irony, Bacon wrote the *Novum Organum* in the form of aphorisms, which are deductions or general statements in themselves; and they are general statements from which the investigator accepting them must work to particulars. He says in Aphorism XXIV: "But axioms duly and orderly formed from particulars easily discover the way to particulars." This is clearly the deductive method. While leading away from Aristotle, Bacon is thus leading back to him. In the preface to the *Novum Organum,* he says, "If any one would form an opinion or judgement either out of his own observation, or out of the crowd of authorities, or out of the forms of demonstration . . . let him examine the thing thoroughly; let him make some little trial for himself of the way which I describe and lay out." In the preface he also says, "Those who have taken upon them to lay down the law of Nature as a thing already searched out and understood, whether they have spoken in simple assurance or professional affectation, have therein done philosophy and the sciences great injury." It is not his intention, he says, to disturb received philosophy, which is satisfactory for disputation, or for ornament for discourse, or for the ordinary business of life, but there should be another stream of knowledge, one not alien to the first but allied with it in mutual endeavor for those interested in science.

The *Novum Organum* is translated variously: the *New Instrument,* the *New Organ,* or, returning to the Greek, the *New Organon,* the *organon* being the instrument of guidance or direction in the acquisition of knowledge. Bacon created his title, by which he implies that the *Organon* of Aristotle is the old instrument. In any event, when *organon* is applied to Aristotle, it means his body of logic; when applied to Bacon, his treatise on inductive reasoning.

I   Book I of the Novum Organum

"Man, being the servant and interpreter of Nature, can do and understand so much and so much only as he has observed in fact or in thought of the course of Nature: beyond this he neither knows anything nor can do anything." Having shot this noble aphorism, almost as good as the Greek "Only this I know: that I know nothing," Bacon aims and fires at the fallacies of logic and at the sterility of science; and he notes the inapplicability of the syllogism to science, to which induction should be applied.

He enumerates, as he does in the *Advancement of Learning,* the hindrances to acquiring knowledge and he discusses the phantasms which enter and occupy the minds of men to the exclusion of truth. Such phantasms, which he calls idols, are of four kinds: those which inhere in the human race generally, in which the human understanding colors and distorts the nature of things, are called "Idols of the Tribe." Erroneous ideas resulting from the search by people, each influenced by his own personality, for "sciences in their own lesser world, and not in the greater or common world" produce "Idols of the Cave." Because words govern reason, according as reason governs words, those errors resulting from the reaction of mere words upon the understanding are "Idols of the Market-place." Those errors received by the mind from accepted systems of philosophy and distorted rules of demonstration are "Idols of the Theatre."

The "idols," sometimes called the four buttresses of Bacons' philosophy, are probably original with Francis Bacon. It is possible, but not plausible, that Bacon had access to the manuscript, or a copy thereof, written by the thirteenth-century philosopher and scientist Roger Bacon and called *Opus Majus*, which was not printed until the eighteenth century. Bacon introduces his idols into various other works written by him, including the *Advancement of Learning* and *De Augmentis Scientiarum*.

After noting the fruitlessness of the sciences, Bacon enumerates the causes. There are, he says, only six centuries of the twenty-six over which the learning of man extends: These were centuries of learning—the ages of the Greeks, the Romans, and the Renaissance. Moreover, since natural philosophy had been made subservient to other study, it has been least cultivated. The true goal of the sciences, mistaken by men, should be the grant of new discoveries and powers to humanity. The false notion that the human mind is impaired by close study of particulars and by experimentation has retarded thought. The task imposed by humanity upon itself is too slight. Material possessions and antiquity have been too much esteemed. Excessive religious zeal and superstition have hobbled progress. Science has been discouraged, and advancement therein has not been appreciated or rewarded; even worse, men have despaired of scientific accomplishment. But he hopes for a bright future for science through a new kind of induction which will discover first principles and lesser axioms.

Book I, which includes the essence of *Cogitata et Visa*, closes with a statement made several times in his works that he has no desire to found a school of philosophy; that he was seeking not fruit but light; and that his ultimate goals are utility and truth. A natural history and a systematic induction are the things to be desired. His method of induction explained, he closes:

> And now it is time for me to propound the art itself of interpreting Nature. . . . For I am of the opinion that if men had ready at hand a just history of Nature and experience, and laboured diligently thereon; and if they could bind themselves to two rules,—the first, to lay aside received opinions and notions; and the second, to refrain the mind for a time from the highest generalisations, and those next to

them—they would be able by the native and genuine force of the mind, without any other art, to fall into my form of interpretation.

II Book II of the Novum Organum

Bacon applies his method of induction in Book II, in which he advocates the preparation of a natural and experimental history. Using true and legitimate induction, tables and arrangements of instances must be compiled. He illustrates his method by a study of the form or nature of heat. Two hundred years later John Tyndall, who wrote a treatise on light, commended his method. Book II, incomplete, closes with an explanation of helps to the understanding in the interpretation of Nature.

In addition to its incompleteness, the *Novum Organum* has deficiencies: the work of the ancients is undervalued; the work of his own contemporaries is unknown or undervalued. Bacon rejects the Copernican theory, saying of Galileo's theory of the flux and reflux of the sea, "But this he devised upon an assumption which cannot be allowed, viz. that the earth moves." In fairness to Bacon, however, it must be remembered that it was not until after his death that Galileo's verification of the Copernican theory became generally accepted; and it must be remembered that Galileo wrote to Johannes Kepler in 1597 that he had adopted some years before the Copernican system, but that he continued to teach in public the Ptolemaic system. Despite his interest in tides, Bacon seems to have been unfamiliar with the *New Astronomy* of Kepler of 1609. Although William Harvey did not publish his discovery of the circulation of the blood until 1628, he began to lecture on his discovery as early as 1616; it is almost incomprehensible that Bacon, who retained Harvey as his personal physician, did not know of Harvey's work.

Neither mathematician nor scientist, it is only by virtue of Bacon's great vision that he can be called the father of modern science. The age was unscientific except for a few who could visually penetrate the medieval fog. Of the age, Thomas Sprat says in *The History of the Royal-Society of London* (151): "But in imitation of the *King*, they chiefly regarded the matters of *Religion*, and *Disputation:* so that even my Lord *Bacon*, with all his authority in the State, could never raise any *Colledge of Salomon*, but in a *Romance*." Bacon's England was sorely deficient in scientific equipment, as is the England of today; but he, like the English scientist of today, attempted to counterbalance this deficiency in mental processes. Bacon was aware of the value of scholarly uncertainty and of the need for suspension of judgment; recognizing the need for the greater use of induction, he rejected existing philosophic systems; and he separated science and religion.

Neither did Bacon create inductive logic any more than did Aristotle create deductive logic: for both processes are as old as man. Bacon, nonetheless, did systematize and make explicit the inductive process which had been noted by Aristotle and which, largely because of Bacon, modern scientists use unreservedly. Limited by the horizons of his day, Bacon could not comprehend the variety and vastness of Nature; but he was, as Abraham Cowley has said, the prophet Moses on Mt. Pisgah surveying the Promised Land.

Modern scientific discovery based on the technique of Bacon is varied and tenuous. But Bacon did make, for example, some important experiments in heat and water. He is a seer in psychological speculation. In the *Novum Organum* John Locke found inspiration for *Concerning Human Understanding*. Before him, the Encyclopedists of France genuflected to Bacon as the soothsayer of his age. The Royal Society had its origin in the *Novum Organum* and in the *New Atlantis*. He discredited empiricism, but his demand for experiment—and experiment following some order or method—contributed much to empiricism. He rejected scholasticism, including the deductive syllogism; and, in the development of natural philosophy, he advocated a close study of Nature as a substitute for preconceptions: not new argument but new art; not new sophistry but new science.

Even Thomas Babington, Baron Macaulay, who could belch molten rock upon anything with which he did not have complete historical or philosophic affinity, was constrained to say in his essay "Lord Bacon":

> Considered merely as an intellectual feat, the *Organum* of Aristotle can scarcely be admired too highly. . . . What Aristotle did for the syllogistic process Bacon has, in the second book of the *Novum Organum*, done for the inductive process; that is to say, he has analyzed it well. . . . By stimulating men to the discovery of *new* truth, Bacon

stimulated them to employ the inductive method, the only method, even the ancient philosophers and the schoolmen themselves being judges, by which new truth can be discovered. By stimulating men to the discovery of *useful* truth, he furnished them with a motive to perform the inductive process well and carefully.

The *Novum Organum*—Bacon wrote October 12, 1620, in a letter accompanying a gift copy of the book for King James—contains the same argument as the *Advancement of Learning* sunk deeper. It "is no more but a new logic, teaching to invent and judge by induction, (as finding syllogism incompetent for sciences of nature,) and thereby to make philosophy and sciences both more true and more active." [1] The protection and countenance of the king would, Bacon says, breathe life into the work which "is but a new body of clay." James, in his own hand on October 16, thanked Bacon for the book and promised to read it carefully, "though I should steal some hours from my sleep. . . . In the meantime, I can with comfort assure you that you could not have made choice of a subject more befitting your place and your universal and methodic knowledge. . . ." [2] But the king had trouble in comprehending the meaning of the work and said, "It is like the peace of God for it passeth understanding." [3] Bacon thanked the king on October 20 for his letter regarding the "work which is for the bettering of men's bread and wine," and asked for the king's aid in having men collect a natural and experimental history.[4] On the same day he sent three copies of the work to Sir Edward Wotton, who had served with Anthony Bacon in the intelligence service of Essex and whose daughter had married into the Bacon family. Wotton then promised to send one copy to Kepler. "Let it not trouble you that the way is new," Bacon said in the presentation copy to Cambridge University," for in the revolutions of time such things must needs be."

Parasceve ad Historiam Naturalem et Experimentalem, or *Preparative towards a Natural and Experimental History*, is included in the volume with the *Novum Organum*. A preface to this work is entitled "Description of a Natural and Experimental History," a summation and the foundation of Bacon's philosophy. Only the method is given in this work because he realized that the history would require the aid of many persons. In the second of ten aphorisms of the *Parasceve* he hoped that the voluminous material gathered according to his method might be valuable "for the sake of the knowledge of the particular things which it contains, or as the primary material of philosophy and the stuff and subject-matter of true induction." Theory is to be drawn from a granary of natural history "made to the measure of the universe." An addition to the *Parasceve* is entitled "Catalogue of Particular Histories," comprising one hundred thirty items ranging from a history of heavenly bodies to a history of pure mathematics.

The one "(who thinketh he deserveth to be an architect in this building) should be forced to be a workman and a labourer, and to dig the clay and burn the brick," Dr. Rawley reports Bacon as having complained when the aid that he had expected from the publication of the *Novum Organum* was not forthcoming; "and more than that (according to the hard condition of the Israelites at the latter end) to gather the straw and stubble over all the fields to burn the bricks withal."

CHAPTER 16

Great Renewal of Learning

"FRANCIS of Verulam reasoned thus with himself, and judged it to be for the interest of the present and future generations that they should be made acquainted with his thoughts." In this manner Bacon opens the *proemium,* or introduction, to his comprehensive work, *Instauratio Magna* (or the *Great Instauration,* or the *Great Renewal of Learning*), that was intended to embrace or be related to all his other works, just as philosophy in his day embraced all other branches of learning. "He thought all trial should be made whether that commerce between the mind of man and the nature of things, which is more precious than anything on earth, or at least than anything that is of the earth, might by any means be restored to its perfect and original condition, or if that may not be, yet reduced to a better condition than that in which it now is." His purpose, he says, was "to commence a total reconstruction of sciences, arts, and all human knowledge, raised upon the proper foundations."

I *General Plan*

Published in 1620, the *Great Renewal of Learning* was far from complete; but, much as Chaucer wrought *The Canterbury Tales,* Bacon fitted in divisions already completed and left architect's drawings for the rest. The outline for Bacon's great work was published in order that "in case of his death there might remain some outline and project of that which he had conceived, and some evidence likewise of his honest mind and inclination towards the benefit of the human race."

He asks the king, in his letter dedicatory to James, to assist him "in taking order for the collecting and perfecting of a Natural and Experimental History," and says, "I have provided the machine,

Great Renewal of Learning

but the stuff must be gathered from the facts of Nature." The knowledge derived from the Greeks, he says in the preface, "is fruitful of controversies but barren of works." He, therefore, would have men emphasize the facts of Nature and direct their studies toward a useful end, the benefit of mankind.

In the section "Arrangement of the Work" (*Distributio Operis*), Bacon sets forth the intended divisions of his great work:

1. "The Divisions of the Sciences" (*Partitiones Scientiarum*). On the title page, he says that this section, intended as a survey of existing knowledge, "is wanting. But some account of them will be found in the Second Book of the 'Proficience and Advancement of Learning, Divine and Human.'" Bacon later made *De Augmentis Scientiarum*, at this time unpublished, occupy the first division.

2. "The New Instrument (*Novum Organum*) or Testimonies concerning the Interpretation of Nature" (*Indicia de Interpretatione Naturae*). This section comprises, in aphoristic form, the use of human reason and aids to the understanding in overcoming the obscurities of Nature.

3. "The Phenomena of the Universe; or a Natural and Experimental History for the Foundation of Philosophy" (*Phaenomena Universi, sive Historia Naturalis et Experimentalis ad condendam philosophiam*). In this section, he intended to include "experience of every kind."

4. "The Ladder of the Understanding" (*Scala Intellectus*). Examples of inquiry and invention according to his method were intended for this section, which is but the second division applied.

5. "The Forerunners, or Anticipations, of the New [Second] Philosophy' (*Prodomi, sive Anticipationes Philosophiae Secundae*). This division—intended for use only until completion of the sixth division, and to the conclusions to which Bacon did not intend to bind himself—was to consist of such things as Bacon had "discovered, proved, or added" without observing true rules and methods of interpretation.

6. "The New [Second] Philosophy; or Active Science" (*Philosophia Secunda, sive Scientia Activa*). Bacon had no hope of completing this division, to which all the rest was to be subservient. It was intended to set forth "that philosophy which by the legitimate, chaste, and severe course of inquiry which I have explained and provided is at length developed and established."

One of the most important statements made by Bacon, that concerning induction, is contained in the *distributio operis:*

Of induction the logicians seem hardly to have taken any serious thought, but they pass it by with a slight notice, and hasten on to the formulae of disputation. I on the contrary reject demonstration by syllogism, as acting too confusedly, and letting Nature slip out of its hands. . . . For I consider induction to be that form of demonstration which upholds the sense, and closes with Nature, and comes to the very brink of operation, if it does not actually deal with it.

The various sections prefixed to the *Great Renewal of Learning* —the *proemium,* the dedicatory letter, the preface—and the *distributio operis* are prolegomena to both the *Novum Organum* and the *Instauratio Magna;* for the *New Instrument* is the nucleus of the *Great Renewal of Learning.*

Bacon's fall from the heaven of the royal court to the hell of national contempt was in reality an ascent from mundane trivia to mental treasures. His closest literary friend was the *Great Renewal of Learning,* for which he continued to design antechapels and cloisters as work was progressing on the cathedral proper.

II De Augmentis Scientiarum

Father Redemptus Baranzano, a professor of philosophy and mathematics at Anneci, had become interested in the *Novum Organum.* Bacon wrote to him on June 30, 1622, requesting him to write a history of the heavens and of comets which might serve as a frontispiece to the natural history. In this letter, Bacon says that he was having the *Advancement of Learning* translated into Latin and that it would be completed by the end of the summer. Bacon devoted much of his time to the translation into Latin and employed George Herbert and others to aid him.

Out of this Latin translation sprung the larger *De Augmentis Scientiarum, Concerning the Augmentation of the Sciences,* bearing a Latinized form of the family name but looking much like the parent. The second book of the *Advancement,* expanded to more than twice its original length, formed the last eight books of *De Augmentis Scientiarum,* as well as the first of the six divisions of the *Great Renewal of Learning.*

De Augmentis contains specimens of the cipher writing to

Great Renewal of Learning

which the Baconians have become addicted, as well as of antitheses, some examples of which he has taken from his essays. The work contains no fundamental changes in Bacon's philosophy.

Copies of the book were sent to the king, the prince, and Buckingham. With the copies that he sent to the libraries at Trinity College, Cambridge, and Oxford and Cambridge universities, he sent the exhortation not to fail, out of reverence of the ancients, to advance the sciences.

III *Revised Plan for the* Great Renewal of Learning

Bacon altered slightly his original plan of the *Instauratio Magna*. He noted the alterations in a letter written in 1625 to Father Fulgentio of Venice:

The first volume consists of the books concerning the 'Advancement of Learning;' and this, as you know, is already finished and published, and includes the partitions of the sciences; which is the first part of my 'Instauration.' The 'Novum Organum' should have followed: but I interposed my moral and political writings, as being nearer ready. These are: First, the 'History of the reign of Henry the Seventh, King of England;' after which follow the little book which in your language you have called *Saggi Morali*. . . . The same volume will contain also my little book on 'The Wisdom of the Ancients.' And this volume is (as I said) interposed, not being a part of the 'Instauration.' After this will follow the *Novum Organum*. . . . As for the third part, namely, the 'Natural History,' that is plainly a work for a King or Pope, or some college or order: and cannot be done as it should be by a private man's industry. And those portions which I have published, concerning 'Winds,' and concerning 'Life and Death,' are not history pure: because of the axioms and greater observations that are interposed: but a kind of writing mixed of natural history and a rude and imperfect intellectual machinery; which is the fourth part of the 'Instauration.' Next therefore will come the fourth part itself; wherein will be shown many examples of this machine, more exact and more applied to the rules of induction. In the fifth place will follow the book which I have entitled the 'Precursors of the Second Philosophy,' which will contain my discoveries concerning new axioms, suggested by the experiments themselves. . . . Last comes the 'Second Philosophy' itself—the sixth part of the 'Instauration': of which I have given up all hope; but it may be that the ages and posterity will make it flourish.[1]

IV The Phenomena of the Universe; or a Natural and Experimental History for the Foundation of Philosophy

All hope abandoned for the completion of the *Novum Organum,* the plan of which Bacon had perfected, he continued work on the third part of the *Great Renewal of Learning.* In 1622 he published the *Historia Naturalis et Experimentalis ad Condendam Philosophiam: sive Phaenomena Universi.* The genesis of this work may be found in *Phaenomena Universi; sive Historia Naturalis ad Condendam Philosophiam* (in English *The Phenomena of the Universe; or a Natural and Experimental History for the Foundation of Philosophy*), published by Gruter in his *Impetus Philosophici* in 1653 and intended also for an introduction to the third part of the *Instauratio Magna.* Bacon lists for eventual inclusion of his *Natural and Experimental History:* "History of the Winds," "History of Dense and Rare, and of the Contraction and Expansion of Matter in Space," "History of Heavy and Light," "History of the Sympathy and Antipathy of Things," "History of Sulphur, Mercury, and Salt," and "History of Life and Death." The "first fruits" of the *Historia Naturalis et Experimentalis* are dedicated to Prince Charles, and in the dedication Bacon promises to complete one or more parts each month. The volume contains, however, only the *Historia Ventorum* and introductions to the next four divisions. The last division, the *Historia Vitae et Mortis,* did not appear until the end of January 1622–23, when it was published separately.

The general introduction to the *Historia Naturalis et Experimentalis* again admonishes man to "search for knowledge in the greater world, and to throw aside all thought of philosophy" until a natural and experimental history can be completed. After condemning the ancients, including Plato and Aristotle, and the moderns, including Gilbert and Campanella, Bacon says that his contemporaries should dominate Nature and create worlds.

A. Historia Ventorum

Bacon listed a *History of the Winds* for inclusion in his *Historia Naturalis et Experimentalis.* The former work was published in 1622. The following January he published *Historia Vitae et Mor-*

Great Renewal of Learning

tis, which contains a title page stating that it was the second title in *Natural and Experimental History*. A similar title page for the *Historia Ventorum* should have stated that it was the first title.

Recalling Bacon's antipathy toward Aristotle and Gilbert, one recognizes with surprise his indebtedness in this work to Aristotle's *Problems,* Pliny's *Natural History,* and the works of other ancients, as well as William Gilbert's *Physiologia Nova,* not published until 1653 but which Bacon seems to have known in manuscript. He also found material in the *Historia Natural y Moral de las Indias,* by José de Acosta, historian and Spanish missionary to America.

Bacon opens his work with thirty-three *Articuli Inquisitionis de Ventis,* or "Articles of Inquiry concerning the Winds," and then develops each of these, including the names, descriptions, qualities, powers, and prognostics of the winds.

His apology for the *Historia Ventorum* tends to preclude any exhaustive criticism thereof. The work is disappointing scientifically: agnostically, he quotes Pliny's statement that it is possible to calm a whirlwind by casting vinegar against it. His description of a man-of-war has aroused adverse criticism; he has without question accepted old wives' tales, such as "Ravens, when they croak continuously, denote wind." Some of his experiments, like that of air in a round tower, are interesting and valuable.

What is withheld in science is given generously in literature. "I have seen," he quotes from Virgil's *Georgics,* "all the battles of the winds meet together in the air," and he thus recalls the excellent description by Roger Ascham in the *Toxophilus* of the whirlwind sporting with the snow. Periodic winds, he says, "do not blow at night, but get up the third hour after sunrise. They appear indeed like winds tired with a long journey." Conceding that Æolus sings too much in the work, the song is comforting in the lonely vastness of the wind high and low over the sea and over the entire universe: "To men the winds are as wings. For by them men are borne and fly, not indeed through the air but over the sea; a vast gate of commerce is opened, and the whole world is rendered accessible."

Bacon says in a "Rule of the Present History" prefixed to this volume, "I superadd Titles of Abstract Natures . . . whereof I have constructed a new alphabet and placed it at the end of this volume." Although the alphabet does not appear at the end of the volume, a fragment found by Dr. Tenison entitled *Abecedarium Naturae* seems to fill partially the gap. *The Alphabet of Nature* sets forth inquiries concerning masses of earth, water, air, fire, and meteors, the first four being the substances or elements of the early Greek philosophers.

B. Historia Vitae et Mortis

"To the Present and Future Ages," an address prefixed to the *Historia Vitae et Mortis*, states that, although in Bacon's agenda introductory to his *Historia Naturalis et Experimentalis* he placed the *History of Life and Death* last, he decided, because of the importance of the work to "advance it into the second place" in the hope that physicians might "raise their thoughts, and not devote all their time to common cures."

Anticipating the objection that a Christian and philosopher should not be interested in the prolongation of the life of man, Bacon says in the introduction: "We Christians should not despise the continuance of works of charity." It was not unusual for philosophy and medicine to be combined at this time; indeed, one of the first books published in England, *The Dictes and Sayengis of the Philosophres* (remembered today because Caxton published it) blended the two. Certainly the medicine in Thomas Lodge's *A Treatise of the Plague* often yields to philosophy. But what Bacon inherited from his English predecessors is difficult to say. There are similarities, probably because of a common stream of influence, to Anthony Ascham's *A Little Herball of the Properties of Herbes* and to Timothy Bright's *A Treatise of Melancholie*, which inspired Robert Burton's *The Anatomy of Melancholy*, a treasury of exotic information, some of which is apocryphal.

Bacon probably was familiar with the major popular medical treatises of his day, including works on anatomy, insanity, obstetrics, pediatrics, plagues, public health, surgery, tobacco, and witchcraft. "A suffumigation of tobacco, lign-aloes, dried leaves of rosemary, and a little myrrh," he says, "inhaled in the morning through the mouth and nostrils, would be very beneficial." *A Counterblaste to Tobacco*, published by King James in 1604, he certainly knew; and he may have been familiar with *Work for Chimny-Sweepers*, published in 1602 for Thomas Bushell, probably a relative of Thomas Bushell, Bacon's servant and sealbearer who made experiments for Bacon and to whom Bacon taught the art of discovering and extracting minerals with such success that Bushell became the most famous miner in England. After Bacon's death, Bushell lived for some while in solitude on the island called the Calf of Man where he engaged in the practice of Bacon's principles for prolonging his life and making his body more healthy.

Two subjects were of particular interest to Bacon, as he tells us in the introduction to *Historia Vitae et Mortis:* "the one, the consumption or depredation of the human body; the other, the repair of refreshment thereof." Beginning his study with inquiry into the nature of inanimate bodies, vegetables, flowers, and trees, and the consumption and longevity of them, he continues with an inquiry into the longevity of animals, birds, and fishes. He then passes to longevity in man and the causes thereof, and then to medicines for the prolongation of life.

"The Porches of Death," an account of those things which occur to man immediately before and immediately after death, closes the work. This section contains a vivid description of a dying man with "teeth firmly set, a hollow voice, trembling of the lower lip, pallor of the face . . . , raising up the white of the eyes . . . , a shrill cry, thick breathing, falling of the lower jaw."

"Provisional Rules concerning the Duration of Life and the Form of Death" is an appendage in which each of the rules is followed by an explanation. Like Sir Thomas Browne, distinguished seventeenth-century physician and philosopher, Bacon sometimes committed unscientific sins, but his medical ideas are always of interest: the toothlessness of lions, he says, may proceed from their strong breath; islanders live longer than continental men; hairiness of the upper regions of the body denotes brief life —of the lower, longevity. He approves the medieval custom of drinking a strong cordial of gold, more for the spirits of salt contained therein than for the gold itself; of taking pearls in powder or paste or in a solution made of the juice of fresh lemons; of taking crystals, especially the emerald and the jacinth; of drinking a decoction of steel several times a year; and he says that gunpowder taken in a draught before a battle is said to inspire courage in soldiers and sailors.

Sometimes in the demonstration of a scientific truth, as the consent of flesh to flesh, he cites clumsy experiments, but with misgiving: "There is an account tolerably certain, and with the authority of many names, that some men with deformed noses, tired of being laughed at, have cut off the excrescences and shoots, and having made an incision in their arms sewed them up therein for a time, and thence obtained more comely noses. If this is true it plainly shows the consent of flesh to flesh, especially in live flesh." Consent and nonconsent of flesh to flesh is today something of a commonplace. It is surprising, nevertheless, to find Arturo Castiglioni in *A History of Medicine* (473), translated by E. B. Krumbhaar and published in New York in 1941, citing the practice of Gaspare Tagliacozzi (1546–99) of partially removing skin from the arm, transplanting it on the nose, and finally removing it from the arm when rooted on the nose.

Bacon rejects the belief of Plato that the virtue or power "of generations was impaired, because women did not use the same mental and bodily exercises as men"; moderate exercise, he says, is more beneficial than strenuous exercise. For the prolongation of life, the drinking of water will not help to any extent, and he recommends drinking only well-aged wine and beer. Condiments must be avoided; and honey, apples, dates, and watercress should be eaten. An herb used by the Turks, called coffee, will, if taken in large quantities, excite and disturb the mind. Cold baths should be taken. "The cure of diseases," he says, "requires temporary medicines, but longevity is to be procured through diets."

In all animate bodies, Bacon believed, are two kinds of spirit: "lifeless spirits, such as are in bodies inanimate, and in addition to them a living spirit." The living spirit, which has the "substance of flame," is "diffused in the substances of every part of the human body," and it is this spirit which determines longevity. Although many of the instances enumerated do not conduce to any conclusion, the work is intensely interesting because it is the product of much research—as much as that contained in any of Bacon's works. In considering longevity in human beings, he catalogues these who have lived to be preternaturally old, beginning with the antediluvian and coming down to the contemporary cases of his time. Although his statements are sometimes not correct, his evaluations of the people named are very discriminating. Some of them seem to be taken from his own life: he knew a nobleman who lived to a ripe old age who each morning had a clod of fresh earth placed beneath his nose to refresh his spirits.

In recounting examples of organs continuing to live after being torn from the body, he says: "Indeed, I remember to have seen the heart of a man who had his bowels torn out (the punishment with us for high treason), which on being cast according to custom into the fire, leaped up at first about a foot and a half high, and then by degrees to a less height, for the space, as I remember, of seven or eight minutes." Not without biographic interest is the statement that, if an apple or nut remain in a conservatory of snow, it will months later be as fresh as if recently gathered.

To Bacon's *Historia Vitae et Mortis* the works of Hippocrates, Aristotle, Pliny, Plutarch, Lucian, Suetonius, Tacitus, Valerius Maximus, Petrarch, Ficino, Roger Bacon, and many others contributed; yet Bacon's work is original in that it blends in an unusual manner his varied sources. A blend, as the sources indicate, of heterogeneous but engaging information, it is a work such as only an age transitional from medievalism to modernity could produce, a brilliant age of multitudinous interests. It is the kind of work to which high tribute would be paid and was paid by a man of manifold interests like Albrecht von Haller, the eighteenth-century Swiss botanist, chemist, physician, anatomist, teacher, and poet.

C. Historia Densi et Rari

Thirty-two years after Bacon's death, his former chaplain, Dr. William Rawley, published *Historia Densi et Rari*, the third part of the *Historia Naturalis et Experimentalis*. The most interesting part of the unfinished *History of Dense and Rare* (or *Density and Rarity*) is a table of specific gravities called "A Table Showing the Contraction and Expansion of Matter in Respect of Space, in Tangible Bodies (such as are Endowed with Weight); with a Computation of the Proportions in Different Bodies." Bacon's interest in specific gravity was aroused by *Archimedes Promotus*— published in 1603 and exactly twenty years before Bacon wrote his work—by Marinus Ghetaldus, who was, as the title of his work indicates, a scientific descendant of Archimedes. Although Bacon examined seventy-eight bodies as compared to the twelve of Ghetaldus, his work is so inaccurate that, unlike that of Ghetaldus, it is of little value today.

Bacon's principal error lay in the fact that he did not recognize that the surface of fluid in a small prism is convex. Although his method is inexact, it is not uninteresting. Using pure gold as his standard, he molded an ounce of gold into the shape of a cube, which he fitted into a hollow prism of silver; then, making another prism of exact weight and dimension as the first and placing other bodies in the second prism, he compared the bodies contained in the two prisms. Naturally, many bodies could not be compared to gold because they could not be molded into cubes. The greater part of the work is devoted to examples of expansion and contraction.

The *History of Dense and Rare* closes with a list of desiderata, including "Conversion of quicksilver into gold (?)." At the end of the study, Bacon partially justified his work by saying that he notes few desiderata and gives little admonition because "the latter is so general and extensive, that it is more adapted to inform the judgment than to instruct practice."

D. *Other Sections of the* Historia Naturalis et Experimentalis

The divisions of the *Natural and Experimental History* which have not been discussed but are in the list of titles to be included in that history are *Historia Gravis et Levis, Historia Sympathiae et Antipathiae Rerum,* and *Historia Sulphuris, Mercurii, et Salis*.[2] Bacon knew that he could not personally complete all the divisions of the third part of the *Instauratio Magna* and, in his letter to Father Fulgentio in 1625, he referred only to the published sections, his work on the winds and his study of life and death. We know that Bacon was interested in weight of air and water; such experiments might be associated with either his *History of Dense and Rare* or with his *History of Heavy and Light*. All that remains of the latter is an *aditus*, literally entrance, or preface, to the work. Similarly we have only an *aditus* to the *History of the Sympathy and Antipathy of Things* and to the *History of Sulphur, Mercury and Salt*.

E. *Other Works Associated with the* Historia Naturalis et Experimentalis

A number of minor works, most of which were published after Bacon's death, are valuable as outlines of later works, as experiments made by Bacon but not included in major works, or as works published separately but related in subject matter to the works included in this publication. Some of the works seem clearly to belong to the third part of the *Natural and Experimental History;* others may with propriety be included in this position or in the fifth part of the *Instauratio Magna,* entitled *The Forerunners, or Anticipations, of the New Philosophy.* Only a few of them are considered.

1. *Experiments*

Among the experiments made by Bacon and published in English by Tenison in his *Baconiana* in 1679 is one in the weight of air and water, previously mentioned. Experiments—interesting as revealing the state of science in Bacon's day and his own attraction to certain subjects—are included on the compounding and separation of metals; the "versions, transmutations, multiplications, and effections of bodies"; experiments "for profit," including "Making peas, cherries, and strawberries come early" and "Conserving of oranges, lemons, citrons, pomegranates, &c. all summer." He is attracted also to the "commixture of liquors." A list of "bodies attractive and not attractive" seems to associate itself with the *History of the Sympathy and Antipathy of Things.* A list of prescriptions or recipes, including "Grains of Youth," intended to restore health or to prolong life, can with certainty be placed with the *History of Life and Death.*

One of the prescriptions is called "A Manus Christi for the stomach": "Take of the best pearls very finely pulverised, one dram; of sal nitre one scruple; of tartar two scruples; of ginger and galingal together, one ounce and a half; of calamus, root of enula campana, nutmeg, together, one scruple and a half; of amber sixteen grains; of the best musk ten grains; with rosewater and the finest sugar, let there be made a Manus Christi."

[143]

2. De Fluxu et Refluxu Maris

On the Ebb and Flow of the Sea was probably written by Bacon before 1616, the year in which Galileo published his theory, because Galileo's work is not mentioned in Bacon's study. Dismissing any connection between the moon and the tides, Bacon says that tides depend upon a progressive motion like that of water "in a basin, which runs from one side up against the other," the continents being the equivalents of the sides of the bucket. His theory must, he says, be abandoned if it be found that high water exists on the coasts of Peru and China at the same time that it exists in Florida and Europe. Bacon's theory has not been accepted, nor has that of Galileo; but each is as interesting as an attempt to explain a natural phenomenon and as an example of the many theories resulting from maritime and astronomical curiosity during the Renaissance.

3. Cogitationes de Natura Rerum

Foreseeing that "these fabulous divorces and distinctions of things and regions, beyond what truth admits of, will be a great obstacle to true philosophy and the contemplation of Nature," Bacon wrote *Thoughts concerning the Nature of Things,* probably composed before 1605. He concerns himself with bodies and their divisions, the atom, motion and rest, consistency and fluidity, consent between sensible and insensible bodies, and the dissimilarity between celestial and sublunary bodies. Of small scientific value today is Bacon's *Topica Inquisitionis de Luce et Lumine (Topics of Inquiry regarding Light and Luminous Matter),* published in 1658. As the title indicates, it is a series of topics or directions to be observed in making studies of light and luminous matter: of bodies which reflect light and of those which do and do not emit light; of degrees and colors of light; and of the affinities and oppositions of light. "As the nature of things leads the way," Bacon said, he will add to the topics. He again implies that the facts of Nature will solve the enigma of the universe and create a true and vital philosophy.

All his earlier studies of the magnet Bacon brought together, Dr. Rawley tells us, during the last five years of his life. The *In-*

Great Renewal of Learning

quisitio de Magnete (*Inquiry concerning the Magnet*), published by Rawley in 1658, is of little significance today.

4. Sylva Sylvarum: *or* A Natural History

"Natural History is the world as God made it, and not as man made it," Dr. William Rawley says in his address to the reader in his 1627 publication of the *Sylva Sylvarum*, "for that it hath nothing of imagination." *Silva* or *sylva* (forest trees, or wood, or grove, or the flora thereof) becomes a pun in the title *Sylva Sylvarum*, which Dr. Rawley appropriately calls "an indigested heap of particulars" which Bacon knew would derogate from "the glory of his own name" if published. But it was published by Rawley because Bacon wished that other men might emulate him and make similar collections. In such collections might be found the materials "fundamental to the erecting and building of a true philosophy; for the illumination of the understanding, the extracting of axioms, and the producing of many noble works and effects."

The perfected history, reduced to method, Bacon intended for the third division of the *Instauratio Magna*. It is dedicated to Prince Charles, as was the *Historia Naturalis et Experimentalis* five years earlier.

The *Sylva Sylvarum* has very little in it that Bacon did not include in other works, but it is of interest because it contains raw materials for the other works. Its symmetry is purely arbitrary, containing as it does ten divisions or centuries, each of which contains a hundred statements that are too verbose to be axioms. The reader is completely dispirited when he completes the one-thousandth statement entitled "Experiment solitary touching the general sympathy of men's spirits." There is little unity within each of the ten centuries or within the work as a whole; the work is a mere collection of observations on natural or unnatural history with occasional attempted explanations thereof. In general, however, centuries II and III deal with sound and centuries V and VI with plants.

The work is also a collection of collections of curious information. Witches and sorceresses, for example, have fed upon man's flesh to aid "their imagination with high and foul vapours" and, with some scientific justification, "when men's noses and ears are

[145]

mortified and (as it were) gangrened with cold, if they come to a fire they rot off presently." Alchemy is repudiated. The essay "Of Gardens" is elaborated. Our knowledge of the economy of the age is improved when we are told that the value of an acre of tobacco is two hundred pounds. There are bits of autobiography like the accounts of his experiments in sound at Cambridge and in France. And there is sometimes charm of style; "For heat and cold are Nature's two hands, whereby she chiefly worketh." A specimen of the work follows:

EXPERIMENTS IN CONSORT TOUCHING DRUNKENNESS

723. It hath been observed by the ancients, and is yet believed, that the sperm of drunken men is unfruitful. The cause is, for that it is overmoistened, and wanteth spissitude: and we have a merry saying, that they that go drunk to bed get daughters.

724. Drunken men are taken with a plain defect or destitution in voluntary motion. They reel; they tremble; they cannot stand, nor speak strongly. The cause is, for that the spirits of the wine oppress the spirits animal, and occupate part of the place where they are; and so make them weak to move. And therefore drunken men are apt to fall asleep: and opiates and stupefactives (as poppy, henbane, hemlock, &c.) induce a kind of drunkenness, by the grossness of their vapour; as wine doth by the quantity of the vapour. Besides, they rob the spirits animal of their matter, whereby they are nourished: for the spirits of the wine prey upon it as well as they: and so they make the spirits less supple and apt to move.

725. Drunken men imagine every thing turneth round; they imagine also that things come upon them; they see not well things afar off; those things that they see near hand they see out of their place; and (sometimes) they see things double. The cause of the imagination that things turn round is, for that the spirits themselves turn, being compressed by the vapour of the wine (for any liquid body upon compression turneth, as we see in water); and it is all one to the sight, whether the visual spirits move, or the object moveth, or the medium moveth. And we see that long turning round breedeth the same imagination. The cause of the imagination that things come upon them is, for that the spirits visual themselves draw back; which maketh the object seem to come on; and besides, when they see things turn round and move, fear maketh them think they come upon them. The cause that they cannot see things afar off, is the weakness of the spirits; for in every megrim or vertigo there is an obtenebration joined with a semblance of turning round; which we see also in the lighter sort of swoonings.

Great Renewal of Learning

The cause of seeing things out of their place, is the refraction of the spirits visual; for the vapour is an unequal medium; and it is as the sight of things out of place in water. The cause of seeing things double, is the swift and unquiet motion of the spirits (being oppressed) to and fro; for (as was said before) the motion of the spirits visual, and the motion of the object, make the same appearances: and for the swift motion of the object, we see that if you fillip a lute-string, it sheweth double or treble.

726. Men are sooner drunk with small draughts than with great. And again, wine sugared inebriateth less than wine pure. The cause of the former is, for that the wine descendeth not so fast to the bottom of the stomach, but maketh longer stay in the upper part of the stomach, and sendeth vapours faster to the head; and therefore inebriateth sooner. And for the same reason, sops in wine (quantity for quantity) inebriate more than wine of itself. The cause of the latter is, for that the sugar doth inspissate the spirits of the wine, and maketh them not so easy to resolve into vapour. Nay further, it is thought to be some remedy against inebriating, if wine sugared be taken after wine pure. And the same effect is wrought either by oil or milk, taken upon much drinking.[3]

5. Descriptio Globi Intellectualis

It is usually thought that the *Description of the Intellectual Globe*, published in 1653, was composed about 1612; but Bacon may have written this work after his fall. He says in Chapter IV that he considers himself "bound not to leave the completion of his history which I pronounce deficient to others, but to take it upon myself; because the more it may seem a thing open to every man's industry, the greater fear there is that they will go astray from my design." If written after his fall, he changed his plan at that time to seek the aid of others.

Like the *Advancement of Learning* and like *De Augmentis Scientiarum*, this work is a survey of knowledge, which, conforming to his usual division of knowledge, is of three kinds: history, poetry, and philosophy. In discussing natural history, he turns to astronomy, with which the book is concerned. (Bacon shows familiarity with the *Sydereus Nuncius* of Galileo, but his silence concerning Kepler may imply that he was not acquainted with *De Stella Martis*, published in 1609.) Bacon's fundamental interest is to determine whether there is an astronomical system, and, if so, whether the sun is the center of it. It is appropriate, he says of the sun, that the "body which has the chief office in the system should occupy that place from which it may best act on the whole system and communicate its influence."

Some evidence for giving a late date to this work lies in the seeming slight regret that Bacon had for his rejection of the Copernican theory: "But if it be granted that the earth moves, it would seem more natural to suppose that there is no system at all, but scattered globes"; and "But if the earth moves, the stars may either be stationary, as Copernicus thought, or, as is far more probable, and has been suggested by Gilbert, they may revolve each round its own centre in its own place, without any motion of its centre, as the earth itself does." Gilbert went too far, however, in asserting that other globes in addition to the earth and the moon "are scattered among the shining globes throughout the expanse of heaven" and in maintaining that shining globes, "the sun and the brightest stars," consisted of "a kind of solid matter."

6. Thema Coeli

A *Theory of the Heavens* is a natural appendage of Bacon's *Description of the Intellectual Globe*. The two works contain reflections of an extremely intelligent man but of one not well established in astronomy. Bacon accepts the tendency of planets to follow the sun, but he does not believe that the earth revolves. The moon, not a dense or solid body, is of a "flamy" nature; flame has a tendency to gather into globes, and stars are flames. With scholarly agnosticism—or even humbleness—he closes: "These then are the things I see, standing as I do on the threshold of natural history and philosophy. . . . I am certain of my way, but not certain of my position. . . . I will preserve therefore, even as the heavenly bodies themselves do (since it is of them I am discoursing), a variable constancy."

V Scala Intellectus sive Filum Labyrinthi

"A kind of writing mixed of natural history and a rude and imperfect intellectual machinery . . . is the fourth part of the 'Instauration,'" Bacon says in his letter to Father Fulgentio. "Next therefore will come the fourth part itself; wherein will be shown many examples of this machine, more exact and more applied to the rules of induction."

Great Renewal of Learning

The fourth part of the *Instauratio Magna* is represented by only an introduction, the *Scaling Ladder of the Intellect; or, Thread of the Labyrinth*. This introduction, together with the preface to the fifth part, was published in 1653 in Gruter's *Impetus Philosophici*. It may have been written at any time after the *Instauratio Magna* was given form. The difference between the ancients and the moderns is that the ancients say, "Nothing can be perfectly known by any method whatever," whereas the moderns say, "Nothing can be perfectly known by the methods which mankind has hitherto pursued."

In the third part of the *Instauratio Magna* we traversed the woodlands, Bacon says, our way beset with thorns; in this part we proceed to the foot of the mountains and to universals. Let us, therefore, he urges, utilize the opportunities obvious and near at hand and, through human exertion, advance true art, which is ever capable of advancing.

VI   Prodromi sive Anticipationes Philosophiae Secundae

"In the fifth place," Bacon wrote to Father Fulgentio in 1625, the year before his death, "will follow the book which I have entitled the 'Precursors of the Second Philosophy,' which will contain my discoveries concerning new axioms, suggested by the experiments themselves."

In the *Precursors, or Anticipations, of the Second Philosophy*, Bacon again urges men of even moderate abilities to undertake new inquiries into Nature. Common reason and popular proofs should not be cast aside, but all men, like faithful secretaries, should record the laws enacted by the voice of Nature. Bacon would not demand for his "dogma the authority which we have withheld from those of the ancients"; on the contrary, he declines to be peremptorily bound by his own work because he would institute a free investigation of individual instances.

As previously stated, this work was published by Gruter. Bacon requested in his will that Sir John Constable and Sir William Boswell examine all his papers, except his letters and speeches. Many of the papers Boswell turned over to Isaac Gruter, who published them in Amsterdam in 1653.

VII *The New Philosophy; or Active Science*

"Last comes the 'Second Philosophy' itself—the sixth part of the 'Instauration.'" Of this, Bacon says gravely, "I have given up all hope; but it may be that the ages and posterity will make it flourish."

CHAPTER 17

Political Strategist and Scientist

BACON'S greatest competence, coequal with that in the law, lay in political strategy and political science, an interest and proficiency passed on to him by his mother and father; his uncle and cousin, the Cecils; his brother Anthony, intelligence agent of Essex, Elizabeth, and James; and by Essex himself. Bacon's heroic stature as literary man and philosopher has, however, overshadowed his writing motivated by his being a watchdog of the nation and also a canny politician and highminded statesman. Bacon's talents in the latter fields create for him affinity with the political scientist, the historian, and the lawyer; but, just as these groups are minuscule numerically when compared to the general reading public, just so has been the attention given to his valuable work in the interest of English-speaking people.

Mention of these works has been saved for this chapter—although they were produced from the beginning of his public career to the end of his life—because it has seemed better to view the major productions rapidly as a whole rather than in chronological order. In this manner another image of a man of varied interests is reflected in another mirror.

I   Certain Observations Made upon a Libel [1]

In 1592 an anonymous attack, presumably by a Roman Catholic named Father Parsons, was made against Queen Elizabeth and her advisers, who were accused of oppression of the Roman Catholics and of originating all the religious trouble in the Western world. This work, *Responsio ad edictum Reginae Angliae*, seems to have been translated under the title *A Declaration of the True Causes of the Great Troubles, presupposed to be intended against the Realm of England*. When Bacon's brother Anthony sent a copy of the work in Latin to England, Francis Bacon replied to it

[151]

in *Certain Observations Made upon a Libel Published This Present Year, 1592.*

Judiciously Bacon begins by saying, "It were just and honourable for princes being in wars together" to contend "by arms and acts of hostility" but they must preserve inviolate "the life and good name each of other" and do nothing "against the law of nations or the law of honour." Then, strengthened by the axiom of Solomon, "Answer not a fool in his own kind, lest thou also be like him," Bacon proceeds calmly to respond to the eight points made by the libeller. Replying to the second point, he says that Almighty God placed "in the kingdom his servant our Queen Elizabeth" and that "the state of this nation was never more flourishing." Just as "there be three scourges of God,—war, famine, and pestilence,—so are there three benedictions,—peace, plenty, and health." England has had, therefore, more than her share of the three benedictions.

Answering the second point, or question, as to whether Elizabeth has been violent or moderate in dealing with the Roman Catholics, Bacon says that she has proceeded "with great lenity, expecting the good effects which time might work in them." The queen has been guided by two principles: that "consciences are not to be forced, but to be won and reduced by the force of truth, by the aid of time, and the use of all good means of instruction or persuasion," and that, when so-called matters of conscience exceed their bounds and become matters of faction, "sovereign princes ought distinctly to punish the practice or contempt, though coloured with the pretences of conscience and religion."

In sections V and VI he discusses libels of his uncle, Lord Burghley; and in VII, red with anger, Bacon replies to the detractor of his father:

> He saith Sir Nicholas Bacon, that was Lord Keeper, was a man of exceeding crafty wit. Which showeth that this fellow in his slanders is no good mark-man, but throweth out his words of defacing without all level. For all the world noted Sir Nicholas Bacon to be a man plain, direct, and constant, without all fineness or doubleness; and one that was of the mind that a man is his private proceedings, and a state in the proceedings of state, should rest upon the soundness and strength of their own courses, and not upon practice to circumvent others.

Political Strategist and Scientist

The rest of VII is given to replies in condemnation of the Cecils.

The eighth section, quite brief, condemns the use of stories fifty years old of persecution against Catholics and of persecutions of the primitive church under the heathen, and of transferring such persecutions to England. He also reprimands the libeller for distorting the dying words of Bishop John Jewel, some of whose works Bacon's mother had translated. The bishop, "the principal champion of the heretics," reputedly "in his very last words, cried he was confounded." In reality, Bacon says that, "according to his life," the bishop of Salisbury "died most godly and patiently" and "at the point of death used the versicle of the psalm, "O Lord, in Thee have I put my trust; let me never be confounded.""

II An Advertisement Touching the Controversies of the Church of England [2]

Something of the preparation of Bacon for the writing of *Certain Observations Made upon a Libel* may be found in *An Advertisement Touching the Controversies of the Church of England*, composed in 1589, published as a separate pamphlet in 1640 and 1663 and included in Dr. Rawley's *Resuscitatio* of 1657. The Nonconformists, called Puritans in 1589, were endeavoring to establish a democratic government within the Church of England. A Puritan zealot, calling himself Martin Marprelate, published a pamphlet attacking the church. Some answers were made by officials of the Church of England, but a series of Puritan replications from the press of John Penry, a Welshman, gave fuel to the religious fire. As all learning and liberality were jeopardized by the Puritan attacks, various distinguished prose writers like Robert Greene, John Lyly, and Thomas Nashe defended the established church.

Strong in his own faith and, through his mother, fully conscious of the Puritan zeal, Bacon wrote in a vein different from that of the envenomed pamphleteers. He sees good and evil in both causes, some seek "truth in the conventicles and conciliables of heretics and sectaries, and others in the extern face and representation of the church." "It is but ignorance if any man," he challenges at the opening of the essay, "find it strange that the state of religion (especially in the days of peace) should be exercised and

[153]

troubled with controversies." He recalls controversies between the church of the East and the church of the West regarding images or icons, for only a pictorial representation of a sacred figure was permitted in the East. He also recalls controversies between the Church of Rome and the Church of England; and he urges both sides to remember that "the ancient and true bonds of unity are *one faith, one baptism,* and not one ceremony, one policy."

Church controversies may be attributed to five things: the giving or taking of occasion to engage in controversy; the extension or multiplication of controversy; unbrotherly practices of persons on one side against persons on the other side; insistence upon drawing partisans on each side into a closer union with consequent deepening of the chasm between the two sides; and unnecessary propounding, publishing, and debating of the controversies. Bacon then discusses each of the foregoing five points in some detail.

In connection with his fifth point, Bacon says, "Love is more proper for debates of this nature than that of zeal." Religious differences should be considered in "quiet, moderate, and private assemblies and conferences of the learned." He ends with the statement that he has set down his ideas with "all sincerity and simplicity." "At the least," he says, "I shall not repent myself of the meditation."

III A True Report of the Detestable Treason, Intended by Dr. Roderigo Lopez[3]

Robert Devereux, the Earl of Essex, in 1592 gave haven in England to Don Antonio, driven from his Portuguese throne by King Philip. Aided by Don Antonio, early in 1593–94, Essex revealed a plot by the personal physician of the queen, a person of Portuguese extraction, to poison the queen. The king of Spain had promised a large sum to Lopez for the execution. A search of the house of Lopez revealing no incriminating evidence, the queen said that Essex was "a rash and temerarious youth." Essex characteristically hid away for two days, after which he gathered abundant evidence on which Lopez was convicted on February 28, 1594, according to the modern calendar. Present at the trial, Bacon drew up a true report of the case, but his report was not published until 1657 in the *Resuscitatio*. The reason for collecting the materials and for writing the report is not now ascertainable, but it did enhance Bacon's reputation as a lawyer. A subtitle says that the work was penned "during the queen's life," conjectured to be about March 20, 1594.

In his report, Bacon gives the causes of the conspiracy and the major characters connected with it. Through the use of the best evidence and sound logic, Bacon makes out a good case against Lopez: he did not reveal the plot to the queen; he denied but later admitted having conferences with spies who had previously confessed; he left the reward in Antwerp, where he was to pick it up and flee to the protection of a relative in Constantinople.

Another such attempt to poison the queen is set forth in "A Letter Written out of England to an English Gentleman Remaining in Padua" in 1599. Edward Squire, an actor, had at this time been executed for the conspiracy; Richard Walpoole, a Jesuit, was said to have arranged the plot. Some excellent authorities believe the letter to have been written by Bacon although they have only internal evidence to arrive at such a conclusion. The style, however, seems quite different from the usual style of Bacon and from that contained in the report of the treason of Dr. Lopez.[4]

IV A Brief Discourse Touching the Happy Union of the Kingdoms of England and Scotland [5]

With the coming of James to the throne of England in 1603, Bacon was aware of the king's desire to unite England and Scotland—a desire that was also his own. In that year, therefore, he published *A Brief Discourse*, which he "dedicated in private to His Majesty." In this work Bacon notes that one sees union everywhere in Nature and one sees that, by uniting, various things receive strength: "waters and liquors in small quantity do easily putrefy and corrupt; but in large quantity subsist long, by reason of the strength they receive by union." Machiavelli, or Nicholas Machiavel as Bacon calls him, when asked to give the reason for the growth of the Roman empire, said that "the state did so easily compound and incorporate with strangers." Union may exist, Bacon says, in name, when it is but a superficial matter; in language, there is no application in this discussion because that of England and Scotland is the same; in laws, there should be uniformity in the two countries of the principal laws, both civil and ecclesiastical; and in employments, these should be blended in time just as "in liquors, those mixtures which are at the first troubled, grow after clear and settled by the benefit of rest and time."

V Certain Considerations Touching the Better Pacification and Edification of the Church of England [6]

After dedicating *Certain Considerations* to the king, Bacon opens with the statement, "The unity of your Church, excellent Sovereign, is a thing no less precious than the union of your kingdoms." This work, first published in 1604 and again in 1641, was undertaken to adjust religious difficulties and to consider the objections of the Puritans to the ceremonies of the Church of England.

As for the use of one form in the church, he says that God left to church government, as well as to civil government, the right to vary according to time, place, and accidents. He, however, advocates the return to one faith, one baptism—and not to one hierarchy, one discipline. Other points made by Bacon include the following:

(1) He approves of church government by bishops, but such government should accept the advice of others.

(2) Private baptism by women and laymen he thought unwarranted by the practice of the primitive church.

(3) The ministry should be comprised of men of learning who have the ability to preach.

(4) He would deny non-residence livings to ministers; and he would reform plurality of living.

The Hampton Court conference, which first met with the king on January 14, 1604, adopted several of Bacon's suggested reforms. When the Puritans objected two days later to the ceremonies in the Book of Common Prayer, the king demanded that they point out wherein the ceremonies violated the law of God; when the Puritans could not do so, it was decided to retain them.

On January 16 also it was decided to make a uniform translation of the Bible. Bacon seemingly had nothing to do with the King James. As if to express his thanks, Bacon immediately began Hampton Court conference, it is understandable that some of

Political Strategist and Scientist

Bacon's champions offer him as the genius in the making of that version of the Bible.

VI Certain Articles or Considerations Touching the Union of the Kingdoms of England and Scotland [7]

Under Queen Elizabeth, Bacon served as a member of the learned council by verbal order of the queen; in August of 1604, however, he was dignified by the grant of a patent to the office by King James. As if to express his thanks, Bacon immediately began to consider the problems involved in the union of the kingdoms—problems not adjusted for a century. Immediately after the title, he states that the articles were "collected and dispersed for His Majesty's better service." "I presumed at your Majestys' first entrance to write a few lines, indeed scholastically and speculatively, and not actively or politicly," Bacon begins. Now that the king has declared his intention and now that Bacon was the first to be selected by the House of Commons to serve the cause, he feels that he may not "neglect any pains that may tend to the furtherance of so excellent a work."

Bacon's analysis includes all the major problems: whether statutes intended exclusively for Scotland should be repealed; what laws of both realms should be repealed, particularly those governing the borders, or marches, of the nations; the two nations, he points out, are already united in sovereignty and subjection, religion, continent, language, and now in confederacies. But there are external indicia which continue a separation: ceremonial and material crowns, names and appellations, prints of seals, and stamps of coins. And there are internal points of separation: parliaments, counsels, officers, nobility, laws, justice, finance, admiralty, freedoms and liberties, and taxes and imposts. The newly dignified member of the learned council closes: "I most humbly pray your Majesty in this which is done to pardon my errors, and to cover them with my good intention and meaning, and desire I have to do your Majesty service."

In *Certain Articles* Bacon recommended that the new title of the king and the names of the nations to be used be announced by royal proclamation. Bacon then drafted a proclamation, not used, in which the "stile and title of King of Great Britany, France, and Ireland" was to be used.[8]

VII Certain Considerations Touching the Plantation in Ireland [9]

In 1606 various questions sprang up as to the jurisdiction of the King's Bench and the Council in the Marches, or the Council of Wales. It is probable that, as an attorney for one of the parties, Bacon wrote memoranda on the subject; and it is also probable that he offered suggestions for the settlement of the dispute.[10] With more certainty we can associate Bacon with attempts to bring to obedience the northern parts of Ireland. The paper, dedicated to the king and published in the *Resuscitatio*, is dated 1606; but it is more likely that the date is 1608 or the first of 1609.

"God hath reserved to your Majesty's times two works," Bacon begins, "the union and the plantation of kingdoms." The plantation of "great and noble parts of the island of Ireland" will redound to the honor of the king. With peace, excess population of England and Scotland may be moved to Ireland, a procedure that may "prevent many seeds of future perturbations." Hostile attempts to invade and colonize the island of Ireland will be thwarted. Fourth and last, through such colonization riches and power will come to King James.

The Prince of Wales should add to his titles the "earldom of Ulster." Nobility and knighthood should be established there. Having said that "all men are drawn into actions by three things, —pleasure, honour, and profit," Bacon closes this section with the statement, "Thus much for honour." As for profit, it will consist in three parts: good rates to the undertakers or improvers of the land; greater liberties; and "ease of charge" or government financial aid. Bacon suggests that construction for the public should be undertaken at public expense.

A commission should be created for the plantation, and the commission should for certain periods have headquarters in some "habitable town of Ireland" near the plantation, and such commission should have a counterpart in a council of plantation in England.

"Thus I have expressed to your Majesty," he closes "those simple and weak cogitations which I have had in myself."

VIII An Advertisement Touching An Holy War[11]

The recommendations by Bacon that King James assemble Parliament for the discussion of financial problems and the numerous memoranda gathered by Bacon for the use of the king in addressing Parliament are important and character revealing, but they must yield their place to more important works. In 1617 the king discussed the propriety of the marriage of Prince Charles with the Infanta of Spain, a marriage that would relieve financial worries of James. Members of the council agreed that he might honorably approve the marriage, but it seems that all persons in close association with the king hoped that negotiations, once made, might be broken off honorably. Bacon probably was in this group. On March 23, 1617, Bacon wrote instructions to be given by the king to Sir John Digby, who was about to leave for Spain, to arrange the marriage.

In 1622, when *An Holy War* was written, conditions with Spain were much as they had been in 1617: negotiations for the marriage had been renewed, and the pirates of Tunis and Algiers continued to harass shipping. Bacon in 1617 had said that the proposed marriage might be "for the good and happiness of the Christian world," but he hurriedly recommended that the pirates of North Africa be exterminated as "common enemies of mankind," and that "a holy war against the Turk" be undertaken, with a view to destruction of "the Grand Signor's navy," which would "starve Constantinople, and thereby" throw "those provinces into mutiny and insurrection." The mention of warfare with two enemies was designed to attract the attention of the king and to be considered as preliminary to the marriage, which might, or might not, preclude warfare with Spain.

An Holy War, not completed, was first published with other works in *Certain Miscellany Works of the Right Honourable Francis Lo. Verulam, Viscount St. Alban*, in 1629. Translated into Latin at Bacon's request, it was included in *Opera Moralia et Civilia*, 1638, for which Rawley wrote the preface. In the dedication to Bacon's friend Lancelot Andrews, lord bishop of Winchester, Bacon says that he would be like Demosthenes, Cicero, and Seneca, who, though banished as he had been, occupied their time and their pens.

He then discusses his plans for writing: he hopes to write new parts of the *Instauratio Magna* and, in addition, because "it flies too high over men's heads," he will rewrite "so abstruse an argument" and bring "it down to the sense, by some patterns of a Natural Story and Inquisition." The *Advancement of Learning* he will have translated into Latin, "the general language," with "great and ample additions and enrichment," and will use it "in lieu of the first part of the Instauration." He will continue "a work touching Laws, propounding a character of Justice." Because he finds that a compilation of the laws of the nation will require much assistance, he has "laid it aside." He will continue to write essays. Regretting that the works which he has published and those which he has in hand "went all into the city, and none into the temple," he hopes to "make oblation" by writing *An Holy War*, "an argument mixt of religious and civil considerations; and likewise mixt between contemplative and active."

In *An Holy War* Bacon uses dialogue for the first time in a nondramatic work; although he uses it with skill, his dialogue lacks the delicacy of that of Plato, from whom he undoubtedly learned the technique although a number of his contemporaries were using it. Bacon characterizes the six dialogists as follows: "Eusebius beareth the character of a Moderate Divine. Gamaliel of a Protestant Zelant. Zebedaeus of a Romish Catholic Zelant. Martius of a Militar Man. Eupolis of a Politique. Pollio of a Courtier."

The names of the dialogists come from the Bible, mythology, or history; and, good Greek scholar that he was, Bacon sometimes coins them, and does so more intelligently than did many of his contemporaries. *Eusebian* means godly or pious; there were two bishops named Eusebius: one was the bishop of Nicomedia and later of Constantinople; the other, Eusebius Pamphill, the bishop of Caesarea, was called "the father of church history." The proper name *Gamaliel* means God is avenger; a prince in Exodus bears that name. *Zebedaeus* means gift of Jehovah; Zebedee was the father of James and John, disciples of Christ. *Martius* means Mars or pertaining to Mars, the god of war whose temple was on the Campus Martius, or Field of Mars. There was an Athenian dramatic poet named Eupolis who died about 411 B.C.; it is probable, however, that Bacon coined the name from the prefix *eu-*, mean-

Political Strategist and Scientist

ing agreeable, good, or well, and *polis,* meaning city in the Greek. In French history the Politique, as Bacon puts it, endeavored to reconcile the Huguenots and the Roman Catholics. In Latin, *aulicus* means Pollio; the Greek *aulē,* or English *aula,* means a court open to the air; *Pollio,* therefore, may mean a courtier. In this work Bacon may have allegory in which some of his contemporaries are mirrored.

The illustrious group of dialogists met at the house of Eupolis in Paris. Pollio begins the conversation: "Here be four of you, I think were able to make a good World; for you are as differing as the four Elements, and yet you are friends. As for Eupolis, because he is temperate and without passion, he may be the Fifth Essence." "We were speaking of the affairs of Christendom at this day," Eupolis replies; "wherein we would be glad also to have your opinion." The man of war, Martius, says that "Christian princes and potentates are . . . wanting to the propagation of the Faith by their arms." Pollio asks all of them what they say "to the extirpation of the Moors of Valentia," and Martius somewhat later observes that nothing could bring more greatness and honor than "a war upon infidels." It was not, he said, for the propagation of the Christian faith that Peru and Chile and other such places were colonized, but for "gold and silver and temporal profit and glory." And then quite skillfully Bacon, using the speech of Martius, says, "A war upon the Turk is more worthy than upon any other gentiles, infidels, or savages."

All assenting, Eupolis divided the whole question of warfare into various parts and asked Zebedaeus to handle the question of warfare for the propagation of the Christian faith. Zebedaeus then asked several questions as to whether it be lawful:

1. For Christian states to make invasive war for the propagation of the faith,
2. To invade for the purpose of recovering church property for the purpose of restoring it,
3. To invade to release Christians from servitude to infidels,
4. To invade to recover holy places like the Holy City and Sepulchre,
5. To avenge or vindicate blasphemies against the Deity, and
6. To prosecute a holy war with attendant expulsion of people or forcing of consciences.

Zebedaeus paused in the hope that others would talk; but, as none did so and they indicated that they wished him to continue, he did so: "As the cause of a war ought to be just, so the justice of that cause ought to be evident; not obscure, not scrupulous." "A war against the Turk is lawful," he went on, "both by the laws of Nature and nations, and by the law divine, which is the perfection of the other two." The rather brilliant, spontaneous monologue of Zebedaeus follows, during the course of which he discusses the pirates of Tunis and Algiers: "It was never doubted but a war upon pirates may be lawfully made by any nation, though not infested or violated by them."

How far Bacon would have gone in justifying war had the work been completed is uncertain. With six persons engaged in the dialogue, however, he probably intended to exhaust the subject. There is not much indication about Bacon's feeling concerning holy warfare, but he says in *Considerations Touching a War with Spain*, written two years later, that offensive holy wars should seldom, or never, be approved.

An Holy War is invaluable as a work of literature and as a bit of history. It may contain unmined allegorical ore. It reveals Bacon as a scholar in history, in mythology, and in the Greek language. It lays a solid footing of rock for *Considerations Touching a War with Spain*, and it reflects the author's political acumen and real power at the royal court. Geographically, in references to Peru and Chile and the Incas, and rhetorically, mellow and majestic as it is, it prepares for the *New Atlantis*. But *An Holy War* looks not only ahead but also back: there can be no question of Bacon's knowing the 1561 translation of Castiglione's *Courtier* by Sir Thomas Hoby, who married his Aunt Elizabeth and became ambassador to France in 1566: indeed, Bacon may even have known the work in the original Italian published in 1528. The dialogue and philosophic reflection in the *Courtier* provided an excellent model for Bacon. But he turned the pages of history back to the pre-Christian era, and he found in Plato dialogists, almost equal in number to his, engaged in subtler thought.

Political Strategist and Scientist

IX Considerations Touching a War with Spain, To the Prince[12]

Two years after Bacon had written *An Holy War* he did not have to conceal his belief that a war should be fought with Spain. The Palatinate had been lost to the son-in-law of King James, and his son was to be used as a pawn to obtain the aid of Spain in the recovery of the Palatinate; but James was never entirely happy about negotiations with Spain for the marriage of his son to a Spanish princess. Spain, moreover, was Roman Catholic, and the English and Scottish people were far from happy about the Roman Catholics in their kingdom who were demanding the return of lands forfeited to the Protestants. The public wanted the king to arrange a marriage of his son with a Protestant, declare himself as head of all Protestant powers in Europe, and make war upon Spain.

When the relationship between Spain and England reached parliament, Bacon jotted down "Notes of a Speech Concerning a War with Spain," which he hoped would be used in the debate in the House of Commons on March 1, 1624. The notes assert that "All will advise the King not to entertain further a treaty wherein he hath been so manifestly and so long deluded" and that "There cannot be a more just quarrel by the laws both of nature and nations than for the recovery of the ancient patrimony of the King's children gotten from them by an usurping sword and an insidious treaty." "The Spaniard," Bacon continues, "where he once gets in will seldom or never be got out again." Among his arguments for making warfare are: Spain "is a nation thin sown of men"; the treasure of Spain is in the Indies, which easily can be separated from the mother nation; a war with Spain would be "restorative and enriching" and not consuming if prosecuted rapidly; and Spain is being weakened by her struggles for territory with France, Portugal, and other powers.

Considerations Touching a War with Spain, published as a separate pamphlet in 1629, was included in the same year by Dr. Rawley in his collection of miscellaneous works of Bacon. A section which completes the work and deals with "designs and enterprises" was not then published. The work was dedicated to Prince Charles: "It was a Charles that brought the empire first into

France; a Charles that brought it first into Spain; why should not Great Britain have his turn?"

"To a war," he says, "are required a just quarrel; sufficient forces and provisions; and a prudent choice of the designs." The grounds for declaring war on Spain are "The recovery of the Palatinate. A just fear of the subversion of our civil estate. A just fear of the subversion of our Church and religion." Bacon closes the first section, which discusses the justification of the quarrel, with the announcement that he will next show what the king may do. "The second main part . . . is the balance of forces between Spain and us." Bacon says that whenever there was conflict with Spain, the English "have perpetually come off with honour," and he gives numerous examples.

In a separate section he says that "the greatness of Spain is built upon four pillars: 1. A veteran army. 2. A profession of the Catholics in all parts. 3. The treasure of the Indies. 4. The strait alliance of the House of Austria, which is possessed of the Empire." Against each of these facts he sets forth four expedients which neutralize the power of each. But he says that he has little hope of doing much about the fourth because the Pope, by whose papal bull the Empire was established, will not consent to free it. If, however, the first three pillars be shaken, the fourth is but "a weak support to the greatness of Spain."

Considerations Touching a War with Spain, composed in 1624, two years before his death, was Bacon's last work in politics and statesmanship.

CHAPTER 18

Man of Law

NO period in Bacon's adult life is without study, speech, and writing on the law. He served as a member of the learned council of Queen Elizabeth and of King James; he delivered lectures on the law; as solicitor general and as attorney general he was the official representative of the crown and made recommendations and suggested adjudication on behalf of the monarch and gave opinion as to the legality of action; and as chancellor he rendered decisions, but, more important, before arriving at a decison, he determined the direction in which the law would go on the basis of that decision if it were used as a precedent. In every official position he was eager to simplify and codify the law, to analyze leading cases, to unite law and logic, and not only to know what the law was but why it was so. If a law needed change, Bacon recommended one, but only by alteration based on the wisdom of a mature man of law and philosopher.

In the writing about law one finds Bacon's greatest experience and his most profound thought. Excellent attorneys and judges have declared him the most learned man of law among people speaking the English tongue. Unfortunately, Bacon's legal writings and pleadings and lectures are highly specialized works with little appeal to the general reader. These productions, therefore, will be noticed briefly and merely to give a view of the complete man of the mind.

A. The Maxims of the Law[1]

Bacon picked out in January, 1597, twenty-five of the three hundred maxims of the law which he had previously collected and explained them "without all colours or shows." The twenty-five he dedicated to Queen Elizabeth, whom he likened to the Emperor Justinian.

SIR FRANCIS BACON

Like John Marshall in America, Bacon wished to introduce into the law general, maximized principles which would make the law more intelligible and reasonable. His attempt should be related to his statements in the eighth book of *De Augmentis Scientiarum*. His desire was to create a great renewal of the law: in his preface to *The Maxims of the Law* Bacon says that some of the maxims "are gathered and extracted out of the harmony and congruity of cases, and are such as the wisest and deepest sort of lawyers have in judgment and use, though they be not able many times to express and set them down." Even today nearly everyone connected with the law is a facile quoter of legal maxims, a helpful and time-saving practice but also a vicious one because very often there is little or no analogy between the bald axiom and the complex problem. One often feels that the legal axiom, like the proverb and the literary or Biblical quotation, is a frustrating substitute for thought; and one senses in Bacon's meager twenty-five axioms not only the insufficiency in number but an arbitrariness in bringing together ideas and principles that sometimes appear to be more unrelated than related, even though he says that he limits with distinctions.

Bacon's ideal, stated in his preface, is a noble one: "From the beginning," he says, "I came to the study of the laws of this realm with a mind and desire no less (if I could attain unto it) that the same laws should be the better by my industry, than that myself should be the better by the knowledge of them." And he ends the preface by saying that he thought "to publish some few" that he might receive approbation or advice concerning alteration. *The Maxims of the Law,* first published in 1630, was an early challenge to Sir Edward Coke for supremacy in the law.

The language used and the reasons for its use are also set forth in the preface:

> The rules themselves I have put in Latin (not purified further than the propriety of terms of law would permit; but Latin); which language I chose, as the briefest to contrive the rules compendiously, the aptest for memory, and of the greatest authority and majesty to be vouched and alleged in argument: and for the expositions and distinctions, I have retained the peculiar language of our law, because it should not be singular among the books of the same science, and because it is most familiar to the students and professors thereof, and besides that

Man of Law

it is most significant to express conceits of law; and to conclude, it is a language wherein a man shall not be enticed to hunt after words but matter.[2]

After the preface come the twenty-five *Regulae* in the Latin. Then each of the maxims is discussed at length, preceded by the number of the maxim, a repetition of the maxim in Latin, and a first paragraph in which the Latin is more or less translated and expounded, as follows:

REGULA I

In jure non remota causa, sed proxima spectatur. IT were infinite for the law to judge the causes of causes, and their impulsions one of another: therefore it contenteth itself with the immediate cause; and judgeth of acts by that, without looking to any further degree.

The maxims selected by Bacon have some intrinsic merit and have historical interest, but they should be used only after very careful selection.

B. *Chudleigh's* [or *Chidley's*] *Case*[3]

Lectures by Bacon on the Statute of Uses have their origin to some extent in a case in which Bacon represented the defendant in 1594. (At this time Edward Coke had just been made the attorney general, and Bacon was endeavoring to become the solicitor general.) The facts of the Chidley case, when recited succinctly, appear to be mere virtuosity, but they are not complex. The following is a paraphrase of Bacon's statement: Sir Richard Chidley, holding a manor in fee simple, enfeoffed a part thereof to Sir G. S. *et al.* to the use of himself and the heirs of his body by sundry wives; remainder to the use of the feoffees and their heirs during the life of Christopher Chidley, eldest son of Sir Richard Chidley; remainder in tail to the first through the tenth sons of Christopher Chidley; remainder to the other sons of Sir Richard Chidley then living; remainder to Sir Richard's own right heirs in fee. During the lifetime of his feoffees, Sir Richard Chidley died. The feoffees then enfeoffed Christopher Chidley, vitiating the intermediate remainder. After the birth of issue to Christopher Chidley, *viz.,* Streightley Chidley, who died without issue, and John Chidley, he enfeoffed Sir John Chichester, who enfeoffed

Philip Chichester, under whom the defendant claimed. John Chidley, meanwhile, entered the land and granted a lease to the plaintiff, who brought the action of trespass against the defendant.

Edward Coke, then solicitor general, represented the defendant in an earlier *ex parte* proceeding in the case. From the King's Bench the case was taken into the Exchequer Chamber for the opinion of all the justices of England and for adjudication. Involving as it did the alienation of estates by heirs and the entire doctrine of uses, the case was of concern to the crown because of possible forfeiture of the estate and reversion to the crown. The majority of the judges decided in favor of the defendant. Both Coke and Bacon were, therefore, victorious. But Bacon had to wait until 1607 to get the solicitorship.

C. Upon the Statute of Uses[4]

Few of the complex problems related to the use of property were decided by the Chidley case—nor have they yet been decided satisfactorily—but Bacon was perhaps better prepared to lecture on uses because of his connection with that case than was any other attorney in England. During the Lent vacation of 1600 he gave a double reading at Gray's Inn on the subject. Having previously read, or lectured, at Gray's Inn during the Lent term, Bacon became a double reader. The lecture—or accelerated course on the Statute of Uses, as we should today call it—required six days. It was first published in 1642 and was entitled *The Learned Reading of Mr. Francis Bacon, One of Her Majesty's Counsel at Law, upon the Statute of Uses: Being His Double Reading to the Honourable Society of Gray's Inn. 42 Eliz.*

"The nature of an use is best discerned by considering, first, what it is not, and then what it is," Bacon says, as he set a pattern followed by lecturers today; "for it is the nature of all human science and knowledge to proceed most safely by negative and exclusion to what is affirmative and inclusive." Somewhat better at dealing with the negative—as is of necessity the case in dealing with a complex statute—Bacon does discuss the positive and cites excellent authorities on the statute: Justice Walmsley says that the feoffor may take the profits of the estate; the feoffee, at the request of the feoffor, must return the estate to him; if the feoffee is

Man of Law

deprived of the estate and the feoffor is thus disturbed, the feoffee may re-enter. And Justice Fenner is quoted: Uses "are created by confidence; preserved by privity . . . ; and ordered and guided by conscience": that "of the feoffee" or "the general conscience of the realm, which is Chancery."

Bacon's explication does not, to use his words in another relationship, "succeed excellently well," but one leaves his lecture feeling that both lecturer and listener have had a good intellectual workout. In the history of the law these lectures are a landmark because Bacon struck a balance between life interests and perpetuities and thereby provided a basis for freer transfer of land.

The preceding examples are typical of Bacon's contribution to the law of his nation. As chancellor he made a list of one hundred and one ordinances "for the better and more regular administration of justice in the chancery." To his chancery court came the uncle of Oliver Cromwell; an ancestor of George Washington; John Donne; and John and William Shakespeare of Warwickshire, relatives, it would appear, of the dramatist. Had Bacon been many brilliant lawyers, all laws would have been codified and antiquated laws would have been wiped off the statute books; reason would have been introduced into the law; and there would today be no distinction between law and equity.

CHAPTER 19

Scientific Utopia: New Atlantis[1]

THE *New Atlantis*, the most imaginative of Bacon's works, is a "fable"—as Dr. William Rawley referred to it when he published the unfinished work in 1627—intended to be used as a model of a college for the interpretation of nature "and the producing of great and marvellous works for the benefit of men under the name of Salomon's House, or the College of the Six Days' Works." Rawley says in his address to the reader that "the model is more vast and high than can possibly be imitated in all things; notwithstanding most things therein are within men's power to effect." Bacon was creating a pattern "of the best state," for which he had planned to compose "a frame of laws."

The ideal commonwealth is probably as ancient as the longing of man for a life better than the one he is experiencing. From the antique treasures of Greece, probably by way of Turkey and Italy, the *Republic* of Plato came to England and there, as part of the intellectual and spiritual reawakening of the Renaissance, inspired Sir Thomas More to design his *Utopia,* the reveille of the English Renaissance, and Bacon to write *New Atlantis*, the tattoo of that great movement. Before looking at Bacon's work in detail, a survey of people and works that influenced him gives additional insight to his work.

A. *Sources and Similarities*

Like More and Bacon, Plato was an aristocrat and was thoroughly trained in law and in political theory. Descendant of Solon and student with Socrates for eleven years, Plato pursued metaphysics in Egypt. More was attracted by Plato's *Republic* and also by St. Augustine's *City of God,* upon which he lectured in London. (His ardor for Pico della Mirandola also kindled him to write a biography and to edit some of Pico's works.) More, like

Scientific Utopia: New Atlantis

Plato and Bacon of excellent family, was the son of a justice of the King's Bench; and, again like Bacon, he left the university to study law at the Inns of Court. More was only fourteen when America was discovered; and, shortly before the publication of *Utopia* ("nowhere"), some of the letters of Amerigo Vespucci appeared in Florence. The chief character of More's *Utopia* is Raphael Hythloday, a given name having rich cultural connotation and a family name meaning in the Greek "learned in trifles." Hythloday is supposed to have made three visits to America with Vespucci. Confessedly influenced by Plato's *Republic*, Raphael says that the present ideals of conduct are no farther from what he has read in Plato or seen among the Utopias than from the doctrines of Christ. After Raphael had introduced the study of Greek to the Utopians, they promptly mastered Plato and many other Greek authors. Written in Latin, *Utopia* was published in Louvain in 1516, and was translated into English and published by Ralph Robynson in 1551.

Francis Bacon, son of the lord keeper of the great seal, entered Cambridge University at twelve and Gray's Inn at fourteen. He began the *New Atlantis*, it must be conjectured, about 1612 and probably not about 1624, as sometimes has been said. Like More's *Utopia*, the *New Atlantis* has its origin in Plato's *Republic*, but Bacon's work is more heterogeneous than the others: Early in the work he introduces his interest in the drama and confirms the platitude that "Art becomes more delightful when strangeness is added to beauty"; to poetic touches from the Old Testament he adds much Hebraic and Oriental culture, and from these he gets or creates exotic names; and his theories of government and legal systems gradually yield to an even greater interest, experimental science: he begins with a rhetorical crescendo, about the waves from Peru to China, but ends with a practical diminuendo about a desire for a catalogue of artificial minerals and cements.

The dreams of each of the three Utopians who would create an ideal state were transformed to nightmares: Dionysius placed in jeopardy the life of Plato because of his unrestrained criticism of government; More was beheaded for refusing to take an oath recognizing royal supremacy in spiritual matters; and Bacon, impeached, died in loneliness. But each of the dreamers and his friends realized that an ideal state is largely theoretical: Socrates says that he and his companions were constructing only "in theory the pattern of a perfect state"; More closed his work by saying that "many things be in the Utopian wealpublique which . . . I may rather wish for than hope for"; and Bacon's chaplain says the "fable my lord devised was but 'a model'" of an institution for interpreting Nature and that "the model is more vast and high than can possibly be imitated in all things."

For this reason, locale is vague in the three republics, although each author did desire to apply all or a part of his work to his own nation. Plato probably had in mind Atlantis, the mythical continent and the setting also of Bacon's work. Nowhere does it exist on earth, Plato says, but in heaven there may be a pattern of his republic. More had England in mind but the name of his work comes from the Greek negative *ou* plus *topos*, meaning not a place. The opening and the aim of the three great utopias are also similar: the dialogists of the *Republic* first meet at a seaport; in *Utopia*, Raphael describes the ideal island; and in the *New Atlantis* the port of embarkation is in Peru. In each of the three lands, man can attain truth and be accorded justice and live in accordance with the laws of Nature.

The governing class is similar in each work: in the *Republic*, guardians of the state; in the *Utopia*, magistrates or fathers; and in the *New Atlantis,* the head of the family or unit, respectively, the father or the tirsan. Moreover, in the *Republic*, each person has his own work; in the *Utopia,* each a craft; and in the *New Atlantis,* each a science or a trade. But property is held in common by the citizenry: Plato opens to the public the storehouses of the elders; More and Bacon provide the public with all food and clothing needed.

Precious metals are held in contempt in all three ideal commonwealths: Socrates says in the *Republic* that the inhabitants must not pollute "the divine gold and silver of their souls by mixture with the possession of these metals"; More says of gold and silver that no person must "more esteem it than the very nature of the thing deserveth," and he makes iron the standard of value; Bacon's citizens engage in trade not for gold or silver but for light.

Plato does not directly limit the size of his city; it may be "small or great or of moderate extent." But, through limitation of propagation, he determines size, as well as excellence of his community:

Scientific Utopia: New Atlantis

those men who have distinguished themselves physically and mentally may unite with the women of the state more freely than may the inferior. Women and children are the property of the state. More and Bacon permit a choice of mate, and each is interested in eugenics to the extent that the prospective mate may be seen in the nude. In the three ideal states, relationship between the sexes is considered to be natural and necessary.

As respects physical, intellectual, and spiritual development, music and gymnastics, producing harmony and providing the foundation of education in Plato's state, are coupled with physics, mathematics, geometry, and astronomy. The Utopians study music, logic, arithmetic, geometry, astronomy, and philosophy. The New Atlanteans may choose for study any of the various arts and sciences. Plato prescribes the worship of the good, or God. King Utopus permits every man to believe what he will; the citizens of the *New Atlantis* worship God, the ruler of Nature.

Other similarities between the three ideal commonwealths and examples of Bacon's indebtedness to the earlier works are too numerous for inclusion. But there are things that Bacon thought and wrote which form a backdrop for the *New Atlantis*. At Christmas of 1594 his *Gesta Grayorum*[2] was staged at Gray's Inn. In the masque six counselors offer advice to the prince. The first advises engagement in warfare, thus forming the background for *An Holy War* and *Considerations Touching a War with Spain* dedicated "To the Prince." The advice of the other counselors provides background for the *New Atlantis:* the second, for instance, advocates "the conquest of the works of Nature" and "the searching out, inventing, and discovering of all whatsoever is hid and secret in the world" and also the erection of four monuments: a "most perfect and general library," a vast garden with flora from all the world and rare beasts, birds, and fishes, a great cabinet in which will be preserved the rare things which man has made or Nature has produced, and last a "still-house" equipped with "instruments, furnaces, and vessels." The third counselor advises the prince to rear buildings and foundations and to create new "orders, ordinances, and societies"; but he is not, he says, interested in "dead buildings" so much as in "foundations, institutions, and creations." The fourth advocates following "the order of Nature" and "first to make the most of that you possess." The fifth urges an examination of laws and justice and that the prince "purge out multiplicity of laws, clear the incertainty of them, repeal those that are snaring, and press the execution of those that are wholesome and necessary," but the prince, he says, must not trust the "laws for correcting the times"; instead, he must "give all strength to good education" and "see to the government of your universities and all seminaries of youth."

Also forming a part of the background of the *New Atlantis* is Bacon's *Transportata* under date of July 26, 1608, a part of which appears also in the second book of the *Advancement of Learning*. In the former he shows interest in "an History mechanique," but first he has to decide upon materials and instruments requisite, and the method of operating each instrument. Then the work itself is to come. To aid in the research, he must look to the various preparatory schools and to Trinity and St. John's colleges at Cambridge and to Magdalen at Oxford. He considers pensions for those engaged in research, the foundation of a college for inventors, galleries with statues of inventors of the past and spaces for statues of inventors to come, and the need for "a Library and an Inginary." Workhouses, vaults, and furnaces are to be constructed. Allowances are to be granted for travel and experimentation. Collaboration with universities abroad would be desirable, and consideration must be given to maintaining secrecy as well as to publication of the results of investigation.[3]

B. *Setting and Structure*

A haven for the person who would penetrate the mysteries of nature, New Atlantis is called *Bensalem* in the native tongue—possibly no more than a blend of *Bethlehem* and *Jerusalem*, or *Ben* and *Salem*, the Good Jerusalem. The "lanthorn of this kingdom" is Solomon's House, an "Order or Society . . . dedicated to the study of the Works and Creatures of God," otherwise called The College of Six Days' Works. King Utopus gave his name to Utopia because Brutus gave his name to Britain; in the same way King Solamona, or Solomon (the name is spelled in various ways), who reigned "about nineteen hundred years ago," gave his name to the society. The College of the Six Days' Works was probably named not only from the fourth commandment but also

Scientific Utopia: New Atlantis

from the College of God's Gift, founded by the famous actor Edward Alleyn. Bacon had examined the charter for Alleyn's projected college and had endeavored to have the money involved placed with the universities and not used for the founding of a new college. Bacon also seems to have had in mind as the site of his college Twickenham Park, which he had sold when much younger. He left instructions that it be repurchased as a place for carrying on research, for he had found it a good place for arriving at philosophical conclusions.

The location of New Atlantis is vague, and was perhaps vague to Bacon. The sailors left Peru for China and Japan; easterly winds favored them for five months, but for many days westerly winds impeded progress. These winds, though, were followed by "strong and great winds from the south, with a point east." The direction, therefore, was northwesterly; and New Atlantis must be in the neighborhood of Hawaii, certainly north and east of Australia. Atlantis seems to be associated with America, and the uncivilized state of the American Indians may be attributed to the fact that, when Atlantis was inundated about three thousand years ago, only some "wild inhabitants of the wood escaped" drowning. The natives of the New Atlantis know Hebrew, Greek, Latin, and Spanish. For the most part they speak Spanish.

Two decades after the ascension of Christ, the natives of the one city, Renfusa, found at sea an ark containing a book comprised of the Old and New Testaments and the Apocalypse, and others books of the New Testament then unwritten. They found also a letter which said that the Father and the Lord Jesus had sent them peace. Although Christian, the natives allow the Jews of the island to worship according to their own religion.

The first person, singular and plural, is used for the narration of the adventurers. The sailors are lost in the "greatest wilderness of waters in the world," but they arrive on land and are hospitably received in the Strangers' House. While the sick are being healed as though divinely, the governor of the Strangers' House tells them the history and the social organization of the island.

On the island the family unifies society. A man with thirty descendants, all more than three years old, is honored at a feast. Bacon, almost in love with the enameled beauty of his own rheto-

[175]

ric, describes a feast in which "The herald and children are clothed with mantles of sea-water green sattin; but the herald's mantle is streamed with gold, and hath a train." A father of Solomon's House wore gloves "that were curious, and set with stone, and shoes of peach-coloured velvet." Finally the visitors meet the head of Solomon's House, seated on "a low throne richly adorned" and over his head "a rich cloth of state . . . of blue satin embroidered." He promises first to tell the aim of the foundation; then about the preparations and instruments; third, the nature of the employment of fellows; and, fourth, the ordinances and rites.

First, the objective of the foundation, he says, "is the knowledge of causes, and secret motions of things, and the enlarging of the bounds of human empire, to the effecting of all things possible." Second, the "preparations and instruments" include caves, some three miles deep, for coagulation and preservation of bodies; holes in the earth for the burial of cements and for making the earth fruitful; high towers for refrigeration, for the observation of meteors, and for the residences for hermits who make the observations; great lakes, salt and fresh, for fish and fowl, and pools for converting salt water to fresh and fresh to salt, and cataracts for "many motions" and for driving engines for increasing winds. There are also artificial wells and fountains and a water of paradise for prolonging life; houses for imitating and demonstrating meteors and snow and rain, and for generating bodies, such as frogs and flies. Through grafting, wild trees are converted into fruit trees, and fruits and flowers are produced later or earlier than they would be normally. Enclosures exist for beasts and birds upon which various medicines are tried and the bodies of which are dissected to throw light upon the body of man; breweries, in which drinks are brewed of herbs and various meats; shops, for dispensing medicines; divers mechanical arts and excellent dyes; furnaces imitating the heat of heavenly bodies; houses for demonstration of lights, including "delusions and deceits of the sight." Other inventions are microscopes for examining urine and blood; soundhouses and musical instruments previously unknown and echoes and instruments for increasing the voice and for conveying sounds in pipes for some distance; perfume houses; instruments of warfare; fireworks; machines which imitate birds and fly in the air; ships

Scientific Utopia: New Atlantis

for going under water and swimming-girdles. A house also has been created for solving problems in mathematics, geometry, and astronomy.

Third, as for employments: twelve men travel to collect books and patterns of experiments; three men collect the experiments from the books; three collect experiments in the mechanical arts and liberal sciences; three try new experiments; three draw experiments into titles and tables; three study experiments of their colleagues and try to develop things of use to man; three direct new experiments; three more execute the experiments and report on them; and three raise discoveries into axioms and greater observations. In addition, there are novices and apprentices, and servants and attendants, men and women.

Fourth, patterns of rare and excellent inventions are placed in long galleries as are the statues of all principal inventors. In addition to these "ordinances," there are "rites," like the singing daily of thanks to God. Visits are made to the principal cities, where profitable inventions are made public and where the citizens are warned of tempests, earthquakes, and floods and are given the means to prevent or to remedy various diseases and plagues.

After this explanation the head of Solomon's House withdrew, leaving behind the blessing of God. The list of thirty-three desiderata appended to the unfinished *New Atlantis* includes the alteration of features, the making of new species, and the force of the imagination upon the body or upon another body.

C. *Influence of the* New Atlantis

The foundation of the Invisible College in 1645 was inspired by the *New Atlantis,* and the Royal Society developed from this Invisible College. Joseph Glanvill said in an address before the Royal Society that "Solomon's House in the *New Atlantis* was a prophetic scheme of the Royal Society," a statement confirmed by Disraeli. In writing to the president of the Royal Society, the diarist John Evelyn stated: "Solomon built the first temple, and what forbids us to hope that as great a prince may build Solomon's House.... Nothing in that august and noble model" is impossible or "beyond the power of nature and learned industry." Thomas Sprat in his history of the Royal Society says that the

Dutch of The Hague may soon copy a town of the *New Atlantis*. The style of the *New Atlantis* is flamboyant in some places and more than plain in others; the rhetoric is often antique and haunting and wistful—like the face of the father of Solomon's House, which looks as if it "pitied men."

CHAPTER 20

Godspeed, Francis Bacon

"I HAD rather be damned with Plato and Lord Bacon," said Percy Bysshe Shelley, "than go to heaven with Paley and Malthus." To "men's charitable speeches," Bacon had bequeathed his name, and to "the next ages." Another Romantic poet, Wordsworth, who confined his public morals in a strait jacket, quotes Bacon with approval in *The White Doe of Rylstone*. But the Victorians were even more admiring: He "moved the intellects," Macaulay said, "which have moved the world." Ruskin says that he was the "wisest of Englishmen." And Tennyson in the topmost stained glass oriel windows of *The Palace of Art* places "two godlike faces" which "gazed below": "Plato the wise, and large-browd Verulam, / The first of those who know."

"And to foreign nations" Bacon also bequeathed his influence. In his own day he was a close friend of the celebrated scholar Isaac Casaubon, librarian to Henry IV of France; of Father Redemptus Baranzano of Anneci; and of Father Fulgentio of Venice. Cardinal Richelieu warmly admired the work of Bacon; Descartes approved the Verulamian method of reaching conclusions. D'Alembert used his partition of the sciences in his *Encyclopédie*. Because of the vastness of his conceptions, plans, and enterprises, Leibnitz says, Bacon soared to the heavens.

To go "to foreign nations, and the next ages" for eulogy of Bacon is, however, not necessary. Ben Jonson, who lauded Bacon's oratory, said also that "No accident could do harm to virtue"; rather it would serve "to make it more manifest." His cousin, Sir Henry Wotton, who composed the inscription on the monument in St. Michael's Church, said that "children of Nature" had never before "had so noble, nor so true an interpreter." A cousin of Wotton who had acted as Bacon's secretary, Sir Thomas Meautys, erected Bacon's monument as an expression of devotion.

His chaplain and editor, Dr. William Rawley, says that Bacon was much "revered and beloved" at Gray's Inn, and that he was devoid of malice and was religious. His apothecary, Peter Boener, likens him to a pattern "of all virtue, gentleness, peacefulness, and patience." Tobie Matthew, his closest friend, admired "not his greatness" but "his virtue, . . . his whole life and character."

In many things Bacon, like all other men, failed. He was the first to admit his imperfections: the "best of men," he says, "are like the best precious stones, wherein every flaw or icicle or grain are seen and noted more than in those that are generally foul and corrupted." But he believed in the perfectibility of all men, including himself. To have "the conscience and commendation first of *bonus civis*," he told Essex, "which with us is a good and true servant to the Queen," was a fervent wish throughout his life. He desired to interpenetrate statecraft with philosophy; and he believed, with Plato, that the head of a state must be a philosopher. In the *Novum Organum* he would, through philosophy, better "men's bread and wine." In the *Essays* he would inject philosophy into "men's bosoms" and brains.

In youth Bacon wrote to Burghley, "I have taken all knowledge to be my province." Knowledge, much of which is found in books, includes ancient knowledge; present knowledge; and, by projection, future knowledge. And to Sir Thomas Bodley, founder of the distinguished library at Oxford University, Bacon wrote: "Books are the shrines where the saint is." So with his books—by others, by himself, and by followers about him and of his thoughts—we leave in his shrine Sir Francis, closer to us than if he were Saint Francis, profoundly meditating; or, as he would like it, "*Franciscus de Verulamio sic cogitavit.*"

Notes and References

The definitive biography of Bacon is *The Letters and the Life of Francis Bacon* by James Spedding. The edition used for this study was published in London in seven volumes as follows: I, 1861; II, 1862; III and IV, 1868; V, 1869; VI, 1872; and VII, 1874. This work is cited as *Life*.

The definitive collection of the works of Bacon is *The Works of Francis Bacon*, edited by James Spedding, Robert Leslie Ellis, and Douglas Denon Heath. The edition used for this study was published in London in seven volumes as follows: I, 1889; II and III, 1887; IV, 1883; V, 1889; VI, 1890; and VII, 1879. This collection is cited as *Works*.

Chapter One

1. William Rawley, "The Life of the Right Honourable Francis Bacon, Baron of Verulam, Viscount St. Albans," *Works*, I, 3.
2. Virgil B. Heltzel, "Young Francis Bacon's Tutor," *Modern Language Notes* (November 1948), 483–85.
3. Rawley, *Works*, I, 4.
4. *Works*, VII, 144.
5. *Life*, I, 202.

Chapter Two

1. Rawley, *Works*, I, 4.
2. *Ibid.*
3. *Works*, III, 285.
4. Rawley, *Works*, I, 4.
5. *Works*, II, 401.
6. *Works*, II, 427.
7. *Works*, V, 319.
8. *Works*, IV, 445.
9. *Ibid.*, 443.
10. *Works*, II, 666–67.
11. *Works*, VII, 183.

[181]

12. Rawley, *Works*, I, 6.
13. *Life*, I, 109.

Chapter Three
1. *Life*, I, 241.
2. *Ibid.*, I, 258 and 288.

Chapter Four
1. Sir Tobie Matthew. *Life*, III, 73.
2. Robert (Robin) Kempe. *Ibid.*, III, 74.
3. *Ibid.*, III, 80.
4. *Ibid.*, III, 81.
5. *Ibid.*, III, 80.

Chapter Five
1. *Life*, VI, 222, footnote.
2. *Ibid.*, VI, 229.
3. *Ibid.*, VII, 226.
4. *Ibid.*, VII, 269.
5. *Ibid.*, VII, 280.

Chapter Six
1. *Works*, VII, 259.
2. *Ibid.*, VII, 259–60.
3. *Ibid.*, VII, 219–26.
4. *Ibid.*, VII, 233–54.
5. *Ibid.*, VII, 260–62.
6. *Life*, VII, 229.
7. *Ibid.*, VII, 229–31.
8. *Works*, VII, 273–86.
9. *Ibid.*, VII, 269.
10. *Ibid.*, VII, 270.
11. *Ibid.*, VII, 271, footnote 1.
12. *Ibid.*, VII, 271–72.
13. *Ibid.*, IV, 336.
14. *Ibid.*, V, 26.
15. *Ibid.*, VII, 134.
16. *Life*, III, 65.
17. *Ibid.*, III, 149.

Notes and References

Chapter Seven

1. *Life*, I, 326.
2. A. Wigfall Green, *The Inns of Court and Early English Drama* (New Haven, 1931), pp. 150–53.
3. A. Wigfall Green, *Sir Francis Bacon, His Life and Works* (Denver, 1952), p. 62.
4. *Life*, I, 325–43; John Nichols, *The Progresses and Public Processions of Queen Elizabeth* (London, 1823), III, 262; Green, *The Inns of Court*, pp. 71–85.
5. *Life*, I, 328–32.
6. *Ibid.*, I, 342.
7. Green, *Sir Francis Bacon*, p. 64.
8. *Life*, I, 374–75.
9. *Life*, I, 375–86.
10. *Life*, IV, 344.
11. Green, *The Inns of Court*, p. 109.
12. *Ibid.*, p. 109–12.

Chapter Eight

1. *Life*, II, 6–15.
2. *Works*, III, 444.
3. *Life*, II, 16–19.
4. *Ibid.*, II, 19–20.
5. *Works*, III, 413.
6. *Works*, VII, 187–211; Mrs. Henry Pott, *The Promus of Formularies and Elegancies* (London, 1883).
7. *Works*, IV, 473–74, 477, and 487.
8. *Works*, VII, 70–71.
9. *Ibid.*, VII, 77.
10. *Ibid.*, VII, 84–85.
11. *Works*, IV, 463.

Chapter Nine

1. *Life*, VII, 374.
2. *Ibid.*, IV, 340.
3. *Works*, VI, 523–24.
4. *Ibid.*, VI, 535–36.
5. *Ibid.*, VI, 539.
6. *Ibid.*, VI, 541.
7. *Ibid.*, VI, 371 and 373.

Chapter Ten

1. *Life*, II, 236–37.
2. *Ibid.*, II, 255.
3. *Ibid.*, II, 258–59.
4. *Ibid.*, II, 267.
5. *Ibid.*, II, 285.
6. *Ibid.*, II, 286.
7. *Ibid.*, II, 321.
8. *Ibid.*, II, 343.
9. *Ibid.*, III, 45–51.
10. *Ibid.*, III, 141–42.
11. *Ibid.*, III, 143.
12. *Ibid.*, III, 151.

Chapter Eleven

1. *Life*, I, 47–56.
2. *Ibid.*, 74–95.
3. *Ibid.*, 146–208.
4. *Ibid.*, 274–87.
5. *Ibid.*, II, 110–19.
6. *Ibid.*, III, 103–27.
7. *Ibid.*, 90–99.
8. *Ibid.*, 218–19.
9. *Ibid.*, 235–39.
10. *Ibid.*, IV, 116–26.
11. Several works considered in this chapter will also be considered in another context in Chapter Seventeen.

Chapter Twelve

1. *Life*, I, 44.
2. *Works*, VI, 351–64.
3. *Life*, VII, 429.
4. *Ibid.*, VII, 365.
5. *Ibid.*, 303.
6. *Ibid.*, 325–26.
7. *Ibid.*, IV, 218–19.
8. *Ibid.*, VII, 429.

Chapter Thirteen

1. *Life*, III, 79.
2. *Redargutio Philosophiarum, Works*, III, 499.
3. *Works*, II, 235.

Notes and References

4. *Life,* III, 254.
5. *Life,* II, 21–26.

Chapter Fourteen

1. *Works,* III, 589.
2. *Remains,* 78.
3. *Works,* I, 78; *Life,* III, 256.
4. Lambeth MSS, Gibson Papers, VIII, 272; *Life,* IV, 146–47.

Chapter Fifteen

1. *Life,* VII, 120.
2. *Ibid.,* 122.
3. *Calendar of State Papers,* Domestic Series, CXIX, 64.

Chapter Sixteen

1. *Life,* VII, 531–33.
2. *Works,* II, 80–83.
3. *Works,* II, 571–72.

Chapter Seventeen

1. *Life,* I, 143–208.
2. *Ibid.,* 70–95.
3. *Ibid.,* 271–87.
4. *Ibid.,* II, 110–19.
5. *Ibid.,* III, 90–99.
6. *Ibid.,* 103–27.
7. *Ibid.,* 217–34.
8. *Ibid.,* 239.
9. *Ibid.,* IV, 116–26.
10. *Ibid.,* III, 367–85.
11. *Works,* VII, 3–36.
12. *Life,* VII, 455–510.

Chapter Eighteen

1. *Works,* VII, 309–87.
2. It has been thought by excellent authority that Bacon is here referring to English and Law French. (See *Works,* VII, 309.) He seems to be thinking, however, of English and Latin, with the latter of which he sprinkles his English text.
3. *Works,* VII, 615–36.
4. *Ibid.,* 391–450.

Chapter Nineteen

1. *Works,* III, 119–66.
2. *Life,* I, 332–42.
3. *Ibid.,* IV, 65–67.

Selected Bibliography

PRIMARY SOURCES

1. Two or More Works

Baconiana. Edited by Thomas Tenison. London: J. D. for Richard Chiswell, 1679.

Francis Bacon, Essays, Advancement of Learning, New Atlantis, and Other Pieces. Edited by Richard Foster Jones. New York: Doubleday, Doran & Co., 1937.

Remaines of the Right Honourable Francis Lord Verulam. Collected and edited by William Rawley. London: B. Alsop for Lawrence Chapman, 1648.

Resuscitatio . . . of the Right Honourable Francis Bacon. London: Sarah Griffin for William Lee, 1657.

The Moral and Historical Works of Lord Bacon. Edited by Joseph Devey. London: Henry G. Bohn, 1852.

The Philosophical Works of Francis Bacon. Edited by John M. Robertson. London: G. Routledge & Sons; New York: E. P. Dutton & Co., 1905.

The Physical and Metaphysical Works of Lord Bacon. Edited by Joseph Devey. London: Henry G. Bohn, 1876.

The Works of Francis Bacon. 3 vols. Edited by Basil Montagu. Philadelphia: Parry & McMillan, 1859.

The Works of Francis Bacon. 7 vols. Edited by James Spedding, Robert Leslie Ellis, and Douglas Denon Heath. London: Longmans & Co.:

    I (Philosophical Works) 1889
  II–III (Philosophical Works) 1887
    IV (Translations of Philosophical Works) 1883
    V (Translations of Philosophical Works) 1889
    VI (Literary and Professional Works I) 1890
   VII (Literary and Professional Works II) 1879

(Cited as *Works* in "Notes and References")

2. Individual Works

Advancement of Learning:

Bacon's Advancement of Learning and the New Atlantis. Edited by Thomas Case. London: Oxford University Press, 1906.
The Advancement of Learning. Edited by G. W. Kitchin. London, J. M. Dent & Sons; New York: E. P. Dutton & Co., 1915.
The Advancement of Learning. Edited by William Aldis Wright. Oxford: Clarendon Press, 1869.

Essays
Bacon's Essays. Edited by Edwin A. Abbott. 2 vols. London: Longmans & Co., 1876.
Bacon's Essays. Edited by Geoffrey Grigson. London and New York: Oxford University Press, 1937.
Bacon's Essays with Annotations. Edited by Richard Whatley. London: Longmans & Co., 1864.
Bacon's Essays and Colours of Good and Evil. Edited by W. Aldis Wright. Cambridge and London: Macmillan & Co., 1862.
The Essays or Counsels Civil and Moral and Wisdom of the Ancients by Francis Lord Verulam. Edited by B. Montagu. London: William Pickering, 1845.
The Essays or Counsels, Civil and Moral of Francis Bacon. Edited by Samuel Harvey Reynolds. Oxford: Clarendon Press, 1890.

New Atlantis
Ideal Commonwealths. Edited by Henry Morley. London: G. Routledge & Sons, 1885.
New Atlantis. Edited by G. C. Moore Smith. Cambridge: Cambridge University Press, 1900.

Novum Organum
Bacon's Novum Organum. Second edition edited by Thomas Fowler. Oxford: Clarendon Press, 1889.

The Promus of Formularies and Elegancies:
The Promus of Formularies and Elegancies. Edited by Mrs. Henry Pott with a preface by E. A. Abbott. London: Longmans & Co., 1883.

3. Calendars, Catalogues, Journals, and Manuscript Collections

A Descriptive Catalogue of the Manuscripts in the Library of Lambeth Palace. Collected by Montague Rhodes James and Claude Jenkins. Cambridge: The University Press, 1930–32. Supplementing its rich materials on the Church of England, this library has valuable information on families, including the Bacons and their relatives.

In addition to collections in the libraries of educational institutions, like the Tanner Manuscripts in the Bodleian Library of Oxford University, the British Museum has garnered collections containing information concerning Francis Bacon, among them:

Selected Bibliography

A Catalogue of the Harleian Manuscripts in the British Museum. London: G. Eyre and A. Strahan, 1808–12.

A Catalogue of the Lansdowne Manuscripts in the British Museum. London: R. and A. Taylor, 1819.

A Catalogue of the Manuscripts in the Cottonian Library deposited in the British Museum. London: L. Hansard, 1802. Like all the other collections in the British Museum, this is important on a general historical basis, but it is especially valuable because the collection was made by Sir Robert Bruce Cotton, a close friend of Bacon who lent to Bacon materials forming the background for a number of his works.

A Catalogue of Western Manuscripts in the Old Royal and King's Collections [British Museum.] Collected by Sir George F. Warner and Julius P. Gilson. London: The Trustees, 1921.

Like the journals of the houses of Parliament, all other public documents are important, but the following has been frequently consulted and found to be invaluable in any study of Bacon: *Calendar of State Papers, Domestic Series, of the Reigns of . . . Elizabeth and James I.* Edited by R. Lemon (1591-1603) with addenda 1547–79 by M. A. E. Green. 7 vols. London: Stationery Office, 1856–72.

SECONDARY SOURCES

1. Biographies

ABBOTT, EDWIN A. *Francis Bacon.* London: Macmillan & Co., 1885. Reverential in tone but valuable because it is latently critical.

CAMPBELL, JOHN, LORD. *The Life of Lord Bacon.* Extracted from *The Lives of the Lord Chancellors.* London: John Murray, 1853. The author, a lord chancellor, is in a position to evaluate Bacon as a lord chancellor and to compare him implicitly to other lord chancellors.

CHURCH, RICHARD W. *Bacon.* London: Macmillan & Co., 1884. Like the title, brief, to the point, and dependable.

GREEN, A. WIGFALL. *Sir Francis Bacon: His Life and Works.* Close attention to the relatives of Bacon, his education, preparation for government service, and attraction to science and justice.

RAWLEY, WILLIAM. *The Life of the Right Honourable Francis Bacon . . .* , introductory to *Resuscitatio.* London: Sarah Griffin for William Lee, 1657. Indispensable, though laudatory, because the work of friend and chaplain.

SPEDDING, JAMES. *The Letters and the Life of Francis Bacon Including All His Occasional Works.* 7 vols. London:

I Longman, Green, Longman, and Roberts, 1861
     II Longman, Green, Longman, and Roberts, 1862
  III–IV Longmans, Green, Reader, and Dyer,   1868
      V Longmans, Green, Reader, and Dyer,   1869
     VI Longmans, Green, Reader, and Dyer,   1872
    VII Longmans, Green, Reader, and Dyer,   1874
(Cited as *Life* in "Notes and References.") A brilliant scholar in ancient and modern language and literature, Spedding spent a lifetime in research and close reasoning to produce the authoritative work on the life of Bacon as revealed primarily through his letters.

2. Background

CADWALLADER, LAURA HANES. *The Career of the Earl of Essex from the Islands Voyage in 1597 to His Execution in 1601.* Philadelphia: University of Pennsylvania Press, 1923. Implicit in this work is the story of a close friendship turned bitter; it aids comprehension of Bacon's "Sir Francis His Apologie . . . concerning the Late Earl of Essex" and "A Declaration of the Practices & Treasons . . . by Robert late Earle of Essex."

CAMDEN, WILLIAM. *Annales.* . . . London: Printed for B. Fisher, 1625. Aids in countersinking Bacon in his contemporary historical setting.

GREEN, A. WIGFALL. *The Inns of Court and Early English Drama.* New Haven: Yale University Press, 1931. Contains account of Bacon the dramatist.

MALDEN, H. E., editor. *Richard Broughton's Devereux Papers (1575–1601),* Camden Miscellany, vol. 13. London: Camden Society, 1924. The relationship between Bacon and Essex made clearer.

NICHOLS, JOHN. *The Progresses . . . of Queen Elizabeth.* London: Printed by and for J. Nichols and Son, 1823. A brilliant picture of the social life of the Elizabethan era and the extent to which Sir Nicholas Bacon participated.

NICHOLS, JOHN. *The Progresses . . . of King James the First.* London: J. P. Nichols, 1828. A portrait of the social life of the king whose wit partially improved his unattractive appearance and of his relationship with the Bacons.

ROEDER, RALPH. *The Man of the Renaissance.* New York: The Viking Press, 1933. A brilliant book about a brilliant age in which many men were like Francis Bacon: they would know all and be all.

SPRAT, THOMAS. *The History of the Royal-Society of London.* London: Printed by T. R. for J. Martyn, 1667. An indirect evaluation of Bacon as a scientist and an account of the influence upon the

Selected Bibliography

science of the day of his work, with the ultimate founding of the Royal Society.

YORKE, PHILIP, EARL OF HARDWICKE. *Miscellaneous State-Papers. From 1501 to 1726.* London: W. Strahan, and T. Cadell.

Index

Acosta, José de, 137; *Historia Natural y Moral de las Indias*, 137
Aesop, 75
Alexander, Sir William, 53
Alleyn, Edward, 175
André, Bernard, 102
Andrews, Lancelot (Bishop of Winchester), 76, 118, 159
Antonio, Don (King of Portugal), 154
Apology of the Church of England (Jewel), 19
Apostles' Creed, 50
Archimedes, 141
Archimedes Promotus, 141
Aristotle, 17, 24, 25, 26, 66, 83, 107, 108, 113, 117, 119, 125, 126, 129, 136, 137, 141; "Of Tragedy," 76, 85
Ascham, Anthony, 138; *A Little Herball of the Properties of Herbes*, 138
Ascham, Roger, 20, 26, 137; *Toxophilus*, 137
Asser, 98; *Life of Alfred the Great*, 98
Atlantis, 172
Augustine, Saint, 55, 170; *The City of God*, 170

Babington, Thomas, Baron Macaulay, 129, 179
Bacon, Anthony (brother), 19, 20, 21, 22, 23, 25, 26, 27, 31, 32, 33, 34, 35, 37, 40, 57, 58, 77, 79, 89, 112, 130, 151

Bacon, Sir Francis, parentage, 17–19; childhood, 20–24; education, 25–27; as diplomat, 27–28; as law student, 28–29; as member of Parliament, 29–30; influence of Cecil and Coke, 31–33; influence of Essex and Elizabeth, 33–35; new life under James I, 36–42; involvement in Raleigh's execution, 40–41; estrangement from Buckingham, 41; created Viscount, 41–42; fall from favor, 43–45; death, 46
WRITINGS OF:
Advancement of Learning, 26, 55, 67, 68, 98, 99, 101, 106–16, 117, 122, 127, 130, 134, 147, 160, 174
An Advertisement touching the Controversies of the Church of England, 93, 153–54
An Advertisement Touching An Holy War, 49, 159–62, 163, 173
Apologie, 89–91
Arguments of the Law, 49
Baconiana (Tenison), 50, 143
Beginning of the History of Great Britain, 39, 49, 104
A Brief Discourse Touching the Happy Union of the Kingdoms of England and Scotland, 38, 96, 155–56
Certain Articles or Considerations Touching the Union of England and Scotland, 49, 96, 157–58
Certain Considerations Touching the Better Pacification and Edi-

[193]

fication of the Church of England, 38, 49, 95, 156–57
Certain Considerations Touching the Plantation in Ireland, 38, 97, 158
Certain Miscellany Works of the Right Hon. Francis Lord Verulam, 101, 159
Certain Observations Made upon A Libel Published This Present Year, 1592, 93, 151–53
"The Coast of the New Intellectual World," 116
Cogitata et Visa, 117–20, 121, 122
Commentarius Novus, 120–21
Commentarius Solutus, 120–21
Concerning the Wisdom of the Ancients, 38–39, 122–24
Considerations Touching a War with Spain, 162, 163–64, 173
De Augmentis Scientiarum, 55, 65, 70, 75, 109, 122, 127, 134, 147, 166
Declaration of the Practices and Treasons Attempted and Committed by Robert Late Earl of Essex and his Complices, 35, 88–89, 90, 91
De Sapientia Veterum, 105
Description of the Intellectual Globe, 147
Description of the World of Thought, 39
A Device for Elizabeth and Essex, 60–62
A Draught of a Proclamation Touching His Majesty's Stile, 96
Essays, 39, 51, 52, 66, 70, 73, 76–87, 105, 112, 113, 123, 180
"Of Adversity," 81, 84
"Of Ambition," 78, 79
"Of Anger," 81
"Of Atheism," 78, 79, 112
"Of Beauty," 70, 78, 79
"Of Boldness," 81
"Of Building," 81, 84

"Of Ceremonies and Respects," 70, 77, 78, 79, 84
"Of Counsel," 78, 79, 84
"Of Cunning," 79
"Of Custom and Education," 70, 78, 79
"Of Death," 67, 72, 78, 79, 86
"Of Deformity," 78, 79
"Of Delays," 81
"Of Despatch," 78, 79, 84
"Of Discourse," 77, 78, 79, 84, 85
"Of Empire," 78, 79
"Of Envy," 81
"Of Expenses," 77, 78, 79
"Of Faction," 77, 78, 79, 84
"Of Followers and Friends," 70, 77, 78, 79, 82, 84
"Of Fortune," 78, 79
"Of Friendship," 33, 79, 80, 83, 84
"Of Gardens," 81, 84, 146
"Of Goodness and Goodness of Nature," 78, 79
"Of Greatness of Kingdoms," 79
"Of Great Place," 78, 79, 84
"Of Honour and Reputation," 77, 78, 80, 81
"Of Innovations," 81
"Of Iudicature," 79
"Of Love," 79
"Of Marriage and Single Life," 72, 78, 79, 84
"Of Masques and Triumphs," 57, 81, 85
"Of Nature in Men," 78, 79
"Of Negociating," 77, 78, 79, 84
"Of Nobility," 78, 79
"Of Parents and Children," 72, 78, 79, 84
"Of Plantations," 81, 85
"Of Praise," 78, 79
"Of Prophecies," 81
"Of the Public," 79
"Of Regiment of Health," 77, 78, 79, 84
"Of Religion," 79

Index

"Of Revenge," 81, 84
"Of Riches," 78, 79
"Of Seditions and Troubles," 78, 80, 81
"Of Seeming Wise," 78, 79
"Of Simulation and Dissimulation," 81
"Of Studies," 67, 77, 78, 79, 81, 108, 118
"Of Suitors," 77, 78, 79, 84
"Of Superstition," 78, 79
"Of Suspicion," 81
"Of Travel," 67, 68, 81
"Of Truth," 70, 81, 84
"Of Usury," 81
"Of Vain Glory," 79
"Of Vicissitude of Things," 81
"Of War and Peace," 79
"Of Wisdom for a Man's Self," 78, 79
"Of Youth and Age," 71, 78, 79
"Experiments in Consort Touching Drunkenness," 146–47
Experientia Literata, 106
The Felicity of Queen Elizabeth, 99, 100
The Forerunners, or Anticipations, of the New Philosophy, 143
Gesta Grayorum (Bacon with others), 58–60, 173
The Goal of Valerius, 38
Historia Densi et Rari, 141–42
Historia Gravis et Levis, 142
Historia Naturalis et Experimentalis, 136, 137, 138, 145
Historia Sulphuris, Mercurii, et Salis, 142
Historia Sympathiae et Antipathiae Rerum, 142, 143
Historia Vitae et Mortis, 136, 138–141, 143
The History of the Reign of K. Henry the Eighth, K. Edward, Q. Mary and Part of the Reign of Q. Elizabeth, 100–101, 105
History of the Winds, 136–38
Imago Civilis Augusti Caesaris, 105

Imago Civilis Julii Caesaris, 105
In Happy Memory of Elizabeth, 38
In Henricum Principem Walliae Elogium Francisci Baconi, 104
Inquiry concerning the Magnet, 144–45
Instauratio Magna, 109, 121, 125, 132–50, 160
Interpretation of Nature, 38, 106
The Jurisdiction of the Marches, 49
The Learned Reading . . . upon the Statute of Uses, 49
A Letter Written Out of England . . . , 94, 155
The Maxims of the Law, 49, 165–167
Meditationes Sacrae, 50–51, 73, 77
The Misfortunes of Arthur (Bacon with others), 58
New Atlantis, 39, 57, 121, 129, 162, 170–77
New Instrument, 38, 41
The New Philosophy; or Active Science, 150
Novum Organum, 109, 117, 125–131, 134, 180
Of the Colors of Good and Evil, 51, 73–75, 77, 81, 85
"Of the True Greatness of Kingdoms and Estates," 122
Of the True Greatness of the Kingdom of Britain, 38, 49, 122
Of the Wisdom of the Ancients, 105
On the Ebb and Flow of the Sea, 144
Opera Moralia et Civilia, 159
Opuscula Posthuma, 105
Phenomena of the Universe, 136
The Praise of Knowledge, 107
Precursors, or Anticipation, of the Second Philosophy, 149
Preface to the Interpretation of Nature, 38
Preparation for a Natural and Experimental History, 41, 130–31

[195]

A Preparation toward the Union of Laws, 49
Promus of Formularies and Elegancies, 68–73, 81, 85, 109
Reflections and Speculations, 38
The Refutation of Philosophies, 107
Religious Meditations (twelve essays), 51–52
Remains, 52, 85
Resuscitatio, 94, 104, 153, 158
Scala Intellectus sive Filum Labyrinthi, 148–49
Short Notes for Civil Conversation, 85
Sir Francis Bacon His Apologie, in Certain Imputations concerning the Late Earle of Essex, 35, 56, 88
Sylva Sylvarum, 145–47
A Theory of the Heavens, 148
Thesis on the Heavens, 39
Thoughts and Judgments Concerning the Interpretation of Nature, 117
Thoughts concerning the Nature of Things, 144
Topics of Inquiry regarding Light and Luminous Matter, 144
Transportata, 49, 121–22, 174
A True Report of the Detestable Treason, Intended by Dr. Roderigo Lopez, 94, 154–55
The Two Books of Francis Bacon of the Proficiency and Advancement of Learning, Divine and Human, 38
Upon the Statute of Uses, 168–69
Bacon, Sir Nicholas (father), 17, 18, 19, 20, 21, 22, 25, 26, 27, 28, 152
Bacon, Roger, 127, 141; *Opus Majus*, 127
Baker, Robert, 123
Baranzano, Father Redemptus, 134, 179
Barker, Robert, 88
Barnham, Alice (Lady Bacon), 37, 38, 45, 57, 58

Barrett, Hanna, 80
Bede, 98; *Life of Saint Cuthbert*, 98
Birch, Thomas, 104
Blount, Charles (Lord Montjoy), 89, 90, 91
Bodley, Sir Thomas, 115, 118, 180
Boener, Peter, 180
Boétie, Étienne de la, 84
Boleyn, Anne, 99
Book of Common Prayer, 156
Boswell, Sir William, 149
Bright, Timothy, 138; *A Treatise of Melancholie*, 138
British Museum, 109, 121
Browne, Sir Thomas, 86, 139
Bucer, Martin, 19
Buckhurst, Lord Treasurer, 115
Bull Inn, 58
Burghley (house), 21
Burton, Robert, 139; *The Anatomy of Melancholy*, 139
Bushell, Thomas, 138, 139; *Work for Chimney Sweepers*, 138

Cambridge University, 25–27, 31, 32, 33, 39, 45, 107, 108, 109, 115, 124, 130, 135, 171, 174
Camden, William, 69; *Remains*, 69; *Annals of Queen Elizabeth*, 100
Campanella, Tommaso, 136
Campion, Thomas, 53
Carew, Sir George, 99
Carleton, Sir Dudley, 64
Carr, Robert (Earl of Somerset), 64
Casaubon, Issac, 122, 179
Castiglioni, Arturo, 140; *A History of Medicine*, 140
Castiglione, Baldassare, 162; *The Courtier*, 19, 162
Cavendish, George, 98; *Life of Wolsey*, 98
Caxton, William, 138
Cecil, Anne, 33
Cecil, Sir Robert (Earl of Salisbury), 20, 22, 23, 31, 32, 33, 34, 36, 37, 89, 115, 124
Cecil, Sir Thomas, 32

Index

Cecil, Sir William (Lord Burghley), 17, 19, 20, 21, 22, 30, 31, 32, 33, 35, 106, 152, 180
Chapman, George, 62
Charles, Prince, 101, 102, 136, 145, 159, 163
Chaucer, Geoffrey, 70, 108, 132; *Canterbury Tales,* 132
Cheke, Sir John, 20
Chichester, Sir John, 167
Chichester, Philip, 168
Chidley Case, 167–68
Chidley, Christopher, 167
Chidley, John, 167, 168
Chidley, Sir Richard, 167
Chidley, Streightley, 167
Churchill, John, 44
Cicero, 26, 83, 159; "Concerning Friendship," 76
Coke, Clem, 44
Coke, Sir Edward, 31, 32–33, 34, 35, 39, 43, 44, 88, 166, 167, 168
Coke, Francis, 43
"Commentary on the Epistle to the Romans" (Martyr), 19
Constable, Sir John, 79, 149
Cooke, Ann (Bacon's mother), 18, 19, 20
Cooke, Sir Anthony, 18, 19
Cooke, Elizabeth, 19
Cooke, Mildred (Lady Mildred Cooke Cecil), 19, 20, 23
Copernican theory, 128, 148
Cotton, Sir Robert Bruce, 101, 102
Count Palatine of the Rhine, 62
Court of Wards, 20
Cowley, Abraham, 129
Cromwell, Oliver, 169

D'Alembert, Jean le Rond, 179; *Encyclopédie,* 179
Davies, John, 56
Democritus, 122
Demosthenes, 19, 26, 159
Descartes, 179
de Thou, Jacques Auguste, 99, 100, 101, 104; *History of His Own Times,* 100; *Mémoires,* 100

Dictes and Sayengis of the Philosophres, 138
Diderot, Denis, 114
Digby, Sir John, 159
Disraeli, Benjamin, 177
Donne, John, 169
Dorset, Lady, 122
Dyer, Sir Edward, 22

Edward II, 98
Edward VII, 19, 20, 50, 52
Egerton, Lord Chancellor, 115
Elizabeth, Princess, 62
Elizabeth, Queen, 17, 18, 19, 21, 22, 23, 27, 28, 29, 33, 34, 35, 37, 40, 50, 52, 58, 60, 76, 88, 90, 91, 92, 93, 94, 98, 99, 101, 104, 151, 152, 157, 165
Ellesmere, Lord Chancellor, 102
Encyclopedists, 192
Epicureans, 22
Erasmus, 69; *Adagia,* 69
Essex, Earl of (Robert Devereux), 31, 32, 33–35, 36, 40, 56, 58, 60, 61, 64, 66, 68, 88, 89, 90, 91, 94, 100, 104, 108, 109, 130, 151, 154, 180
Eupolis, 160
Evelyn, John, 177

Fabyan, Robert, 102
Farnaby, Thomas, 53, 54; *The Anthology of the Anthology,* 53
Fenner, Justice, 169
Fernley, Jane, 18
Ficino, Marsilo, 141
Fulgentio, Father, 142, 148, 149, 179

Galileo, 128, 144; *Sydereus Nuncius,* 147
Ghetaldus, Marinus, 141
Gilbert, William, 119, 136, 137, 148; *New Philosophy,* 119; *Physiologia Nova,* 137
Glanvill, Joseph, 177
Goethe, Johann Wolfgang von, 111
Gorhambury (house), 21, 22, 26, 40, 45, 122

Gosnold, Henry, 112
Gray's Inn, 18, 31, 57, 58, 62, 63, 64, 77, 85, 112, 168, 171, 173, 180
Greene, Robert, 153
Greville, Sir Foulke, 33, 103, 109
Grey, Lady Jane, 20
Gruter, 136, 149; *Impetus Philosophici,* 136, 149

Hall, 102
Haller, Albrecht von, 141
Hampton Court Conference, 156
Harleian manuscripts (in British Museum), 78
Harpsfield, Nicholas, 98
Harvey, William, 128
Hastings, Sir George, 44
Hatton, Lady, 32–33, 43, 44
Hatton, Sir William, 32
Haviland, John, 80
Hearne, Thomas, 100
Henry (Prince of Wales), 76, 104
Henry IV (France), 179
Henry VII (England), 101, 102, 103
Henry VIII (England), 18, 21, 99, 101
Herbert, George, 53, 134
Herodotus, 85
Hesiod, 123
Heywood, John, 58; *Epigrams,* 69, 70; *The Playe Called the Four PP.*
Hippocrates, 141
Hoby, Sir Thomas, 19, 162
Holinshed, Raphael, 102
Homer, 85, 123
Horace, 69, 85
Hughes, Thomas, 58

Index Librorum Prohibitorum, 100

James I (England, VI of Scotland), 34, 35, 36–37, 38, 39, 40, 43, 44, 52, 53, 64, 80, 88, 89, 90, 92, 95, 96, 98, 101, 102, 104, 106, 115, 122, 130, 132, 138, 151, 155, 157, 158, 159, 163, 165; *Basilikon Doron,* 104; *A Counterblaste to Tobacco,* 138

James, Saint, 83
Jewel, Bishop John, 153
John, Saint, 87
Johnson, Samuel, 84
Jones, Inigo, 62
Jonson, Ben, 42, 56, 179
Justinian (Emperor), 165

Kepler, Johannes, 128, 130, 147; *De Stella Martis,* 147; *New Astronomy,* 128
Krumbhaar, E. B., 140

Lancaster, John, 58
Latham, George, 100
Leibnitz, Gottfried, Baron von, 179
Locke, John, 129; *Concerning Human Understanding,* 129
Lodge, Thomas, 138; *A Treatise of the Plague,* 138
Lopez, Dr. Roderigo, 94, 100, 154–155
Lucan, 85
Lucian, 85, 141
Lucilius, 76
Lucretius, 85, 113
Lydgate, John, 70
Lyly, John, 108, 153

Machiavelli, Niccolò, 155
Malthus, Thomas Robert, 179
Manners, Roger (fifth Earl of Rutland), 66, 67
Marprelate, Martin, 153
Marriage of the Thames and the Rhine (*Masque of the Inner-Temple and Gray's Inn* by Beaumont), 62–64
Marshall, John, 166
Martyr, Peter, 19
Mary, Queen, 18
Masque of the Flowers (presented by Bacon), 64–65
Masque of the Middle Temple and Lincoln's Inn (Chapman), 62
Masque of Proteus (at Gray's Inn), 63

Index

Matthew, Tobie, 51, 80, 84, 99, 105, 115, 118, 123, 180
Maximus, Valerius, 141
Meautys, Sir Thomas, 179
Merry Drollery, 54
Milton, John, 112
Mirandola, Pico della, 170
Montaigne, Michel de, 76, 83, 84
More, Sir Thomas, 103, 170, 171, 172, 173; *Utopia,* 103, 170, 171, 172

Nashe, Thomas, 153
Neile, Dr. Richard, 20
Neville, Lady, 122
Newcomb, T., 100
Nicene Creed, 50
North, Sir Thomas, 105
Northampton, Earl of, 115

O'Neill, Hugh (Earl of Tyrone), 34
Ovid, 69, 85
Oxford University, 45, 108, 115, 135, 174, 180

Pakington, Lady, 118
Pakington, Sir John, 38
Paley, William, 179
Pamphill, Eusebius, 160
Paris, University of, 108
Parker, Matthew, 17
Parsons, Father, 93, 151; *Responsio ad edictum Reginae Angliae,* 93, 151
Paulet, Sir Amias, 27, 28
Penry, John, 153
Petrarch, 141
Phelips, Sir Edward, 64
Philip (King of Spain), 154
Plato, 85, 110, 113, 136, 140, 160, 162, 171, 172, 179, 180; *Republic,* 170, 171, 172
Plautus, 85
Playfer, Dr., 115
Pliny, 85, 137, 141; *Natural History,* 137
Plutarch, 83, 105, 141; *Lives,* 105
Politiques (group), 28

Poseidippus, 53
Pott, Mrs. Henry, 109
Ptolemaic system, 128
Pythagoras, 17, 122

Quintilian, 17

Raleigh, Sir Walter, 22, 29, 40, 41, 86, 89; *History of the World,* 40
Rawley, Dr. William, 19, 81, 99, 101, 104, 105, 125, 131, 141, 144, 145, 153, 159, 163, 170, 180
Redgrave (house), 21
Reformation, 19
Richard III (England), 98
Richelieu, Cardinal, 179
Robynson, Ralph, 171
Roper, William, 98; *Life of Sir Thomas More,* 98
Royal Society, 177
Ruskin, John, 179
Russell, Lord, 19

Sackville, Thomas, 122
Savill, Sir Henry, 55
Scots Psalter, 53
Seneca, 69, 76, 159
Shakespeare, John, 169
Shakespeare, William, 45, 56, 69, 70; *As You Like It,* 69; *The Merchant of Venice,* 70
Shakespeare, William (relative of dramatist), 169
Shelley, Mary, 103
Shelley, Percy Bysshe, 123, 179; *Prometheus Unbound,* 123
Sidney, Sir Philip, 66, 108
Simnel, Lambert, 103
Socrates, 86, 171, 172
Solomon, 152, 174
Solon, 170
Spanish Armada, 34, 93
Spedding, James, 60
Speed, John, 101, 102
Spenser, Edmund, 63, 112; *The Faerie Queen,* 63

Sprat, Thomas, 128, 177; *The History of the Royal-Society of London*, 128, 177
Squire, Edward, 94, 155
Sternhold, Thomas, 53; *Certain Psalms*, 53
Stowe, 102
Stuart, Lady Arabella, 40
Suetonius, 85, 141

Tacitus, 83, 98, 141
Tagliacozzi, Gaspare, 140
Taylor, Jeremy, 86
Tenison, 143
Tennyson, Alfred Lord, 179; *The Palace of Art*, 179
Twickenham Park, 175
Tyndall, John, 128

Udall, Nicholas, 70

Vega, Lope de, 56
Vergil, Polydore, 102
Vespucci, Amerigo, 171

Villiers, Sir George (Duke of Buckingham), 41, 43, 44, 45, 80, 135
Villiers, Sir John, 43
Virgil, 69, 85, 137; *Georgics*, 137
Vulgate, 70

Walmsley, Justice, 168
Walpole, Richard, 155
Walsall, John, 20
Warbeck, Perkin, 103
Washington, George, 169
Whitaker, Richard, 80
Whitehall Palace, 21
Whitgift, Dr. John, 26, 33
Williams, Sir Roger, 61
Winwood, Sir Ralph, 43
Wordsworth, William, 179; *The White Doe of Rylstone*, 179
Wotton, Sir Edward, 130
Wotton, Sir Henry, 54, 105, 179; *Reliquiae Wottonianae*, 54

Yelverton, Christopher, 58
York House, 17, 18, 20, 40, 45